BOOTLESS CRIES

A Memoir in Parts

TOM KEATING

Bootless Cries
A Memoir in Parts

First published in Australia by Tom Keating 2025

Copyright © Tom Keating 2025
All Rights Reserved

A catalogue record for this
book is available from the
National Library of Australia

ISBN: 978-1-7640310-0-4 (pbk)
ISBN: 978-1-7640310-1-1 (ebk)

Typesetting and design by Publicious Book Publishing
Published in collaboration with Publicious Book Publishing
www.publicious.com.au

No part of this book may be reproduced in any form, by photocopying or by any electronic or mechanical means, including information storage or retrieval systems, without permission in writing from both the copyright owner and the publisher of this book.

In memory of and in deepest gratitude to
Allan Keating
Professor Kit Carson
Dr Brian Scarlett
Paul Dominici

Contents

Forword i

Introduction iii

Section 1: In my ending is my beginning

1. Broady Boy 1
2. My Father's Hat 6
3. Snowdon's Guilty Secret 11
4. Stalwart 18
5. Pallotti College Millgrove 19

Section 2: Unmasked eyes in half masked space

6. Juvenile Justice Reform in Victoria 25
7. After the Deluge – some reflections on more than twenty years of disaster management 28
8. Some Issues arising from Disaster Recover Management 38
9. Protecting Victoria's Children 45
10. Indigenous Participation in Child Protection 51
11. A Place in the world for everyone - Mayday Hill Training Centre 55
12. Organisational Turnaround in the Department of Community Welfare Services 59
13. The nursing dispute and its precedents 65
14. Gaming the System 69

15. Joined-up government – a good idea untried 72
16. Health Service Amalgamations - the Albury Wodonga experience 75
17. Maintaining Values in Market Based Care...................... 84
18. The Victorian Nurse Practitioner Program 100

Section 3: Builder not sacker, your shield the mortar board

19. Communalism and Disaster Recovery 107
20. Mental Illness and Compassion.................................. 112
21. Hallelujah 115
22. Multi-disciplinary training for Mental Health................ 118
23. Non-medical Prescribing 121
24. Rural Communities and Structural Change in Health Care 125
25. Incentives for Rural Health Employment...................... 128
26. Improving Health Care in Rural Australia 132
27. The Challenge of Health Workforce Planning................ 135
28. Place Management: An Alternative Approach to Public Administration 148
29. Managing for Place: Some Challenges Facing Human Services Management... 152
30. Tools for Change: The Intellectual Disability Services Act 1986 165
31. Promoting Science Careers in Health 169
32. Hospitals of the Future.. 172
33. Privatising Care... 176
34. Educational Rigidity or Learning?................................ 180
35. Politics and the State of Health 183

Section 4: In Majorca Alfonso watched the door.

36. A Scottish Tale 187
37. Just Don't Call Us Saints 189
38. Abuse in Ireland's Industrial Schools 192
39. The Host of the Air 197
40. Willian Smith O'Brien – An Irishman in Australia 204
41. Travelling North 209
42. A tour around Dublin in poetry and song...................... 212

Section 5: In Retrospect and Prospect

When, in disgrace with fortune and men's eyes,
I all alone beweep my outcast state,
And trouble deaf heaven with my bootless cries,
                        William Shakespear, Sonnet 29

*to break unjust fetters
and undo the thongs of the yoke,*

*to let the oppressed go free,
and break every yoke,
to share your bread with the hungry,
and shelter the homeless poor,*

*to clothe the man you see to be naked
and not turn from your own kin?
Then will your light shine like the dawn
and your wound be quickly healed over.*

*If you do away with the yoke,
the clenched fist, the wicked word,
if you give your bread to the hungry,
and relief to the oppressed,*

*your light will rise in the darkness,
and your shadows become like noon.*

*You will rebuild the ancient ruins,
build up on the old foundations.
You will be called "Breach-mender",
"Restorer of ruined houses"*
                                Isaiah: 58

Foreword

It is a privilege to write a foreword for this deeply insightful book, by Tom Keating, that blends a personal memoir, with insights from his professional experience, along with many literary reflections on his background and Irish heritage. Tom brings a personal lens to his experiences, from his formative years in Broadmeadows, to descriptions and analyses of the evolution of aspects of community services in Victoria, over a span of 5 plus decades.

The memoir provides a thought-provoking commentary on Tom's selected areas of social change in Victoria, and from this we can clearly see the values that shaped his approach to leadership and service, including his commitment to social justice and community services.

Given the comprehensive, insightful, and sometimes provocative analysis of such changes, the book offers a valuable resource for policymakers, practitioners, and anyone interested in the history of community services in Victoria

His poetic reflections on Ireland add another rich layer to this book, demonstrating his literary skills, and his deep connection to his cultural roots.

I was fortunate to have worked in collaboration alongside Tom Keating for many years—through the transformative decades of the 1960s, 70s, and 80s and well beyond— and I have witnessed firsthand Tom's unwavering dedication to the betterment of child, youth, and family services, as well as his invaluable contributions to policy development and implementation.

I was also a beneficiary, through our association, of being enriched by countless discussions on policy directions, community needs, and the ever-changing landscape of service delivery – sometimes including singing Irish songs at management Conferences!

In the book, Tom has selected some of the key areas that have actively shaped the landscape of child, youth, and family services, including juvenile justice, child protection, and regional service development. The analysis also covers areas such as the complexities of managing disaster support and recovery, as well as those of health and mental health services, with Tom always maintaining a steadfast commitment to community-based initiatives and regional development. Tom presents these complex developments with a clarity and a depth of understanding. His ability to translate the nuances of governance, service integration, and frontline realities into an engaging and articulate narrative is exceptional. In his writings there is a deep understanding of policy development, coupled with his exceptional ability to understand the complex and interrelated issues, and the need for translation into actionable strategies.

For those of us who played a role in shaping and managing some of these changes, this book will spark memories of hard-fought battles, the challenges of developing and implementing policies whilst working with different state and commonwealth governments - but also the successes, that reshaped Victoria's approach to community services. For those less familiar with aspects of the sector's history, it offers an invaluable account of how policy is shaped—not in isolation, but through hard work over the years, negotiating and advocating, and maintaining an on-going commitment to the values, and for reform.

This book, as well as being a chronicle of history, is a call to understand where we have come from, to celebrate progress, and to appreciate the lessons learned, in order to continue to develop and improve. The book is an engaging blend of personal memoir, policy analysis, and cultural reflection, written by a man whose life and work have left an indelible mark on the sector. I am confident that this book will provide insights and challenges to current and future generations, just as Tom's work has done so over the past 50 plus years.

Ken Williams PSM
Former General Manager, Department of Human Services

Introduction

The past 50 years has been a time of momentous change in the provision community services, disability, aged care and health services. I have had the privilege of being a part of those changes; sometimes leading them, always participating and always observing them. For me, writing about the world is part of the epistemic process. It is the way I have learned to decipher what is happening and to understand it. Throughout my career I have written about the important things with which I was engaged and used that writing to further my understanding and that of others.

This book is not a memoir in the traditional sense of a personal history. It is a reflection on some of the most significant developments in human services over the period. It is made up of discrete pieces of writing, originally published in a variety of places, that provide a contemporaneous perspective on the events they describe. With only minor edits, they remain as they were written at the time, serving as a historical record of the events themselves, and of my reactions to them. They were written for a variety of audiences; in some cases, for an academic audience, in some for peers and in others, for a general public. Naturally, their length, depth, and clarity varies, but they are as they are.

Throughout my career, I have had the privilege of leading and being a part of these developments. I commenced my professional career working with young people in Broadmeadows and Brunswick before establishing and managing Victoria's first youth refuge and emergency accommodation services for homeless young people. I managed disaster recovery efforts following the Ash Wednesday bushfires and was responsible, with others, for establishing Victoria's child protection services. At the age of 27, I took up a Regional Director position in a rural region and progressively became responsible for all health, welfare, disability, aged care and public housing in the North East of Victoria and the Goulburn Valley. I was responsible for integrating intellectual disability services into the Department of Community Services regional operations and contributed to the major reforms of intellectual disability services that took place in the 1980s and 90s, including the closure of one of Victoria's largest disability institutions. I was also instrumental in defining the roles of nurse practitioners and midwives in Victoria and led the process of merging the acute health services of Albury and Wodonga. More recently, I have worked alongside hospitals and primary care services to develop models of integrated care.

Alongside my professional work, I have had a parallel academic career, holding appointments as Pro Vice-Chancellor and Associate Professor at La Trobe University, Associate Professor (Research) at the University of New South Wales, Marie Curie Visiting Research Fellow at Trinity College Dublin, and Honorary Principal Fellow at the University of Melbourne.

Building sustainable community infrastructure has been my life's work, and in doing so, I have had the honour of working alongside and learning from some of the most inspiring mentors and colleagues.

I take my title from Shakespear's sonnet 29, "When, in disgrace with fortune and men's eyes". It is a poem that starts in despair at current circumstances and rises to a conclusion of supreme hope. These articles are, if you, like, the bootless cries with which I have troubled deaf heaven, with nonetheless, a hopefulness of better things.

The book is structured into five sections:
The first, **In my ending is my beginning**, takes inspiration from T.S. Eliot's *East Coker*, one of the *Four Quartets* that he wrote late in life, in which he reflects on his origins. My own beginnings were shaped by growing up in Melbourne's northern suburbs during a time of major social change, being raised by one of the kindest and most genuine of men and surviving the abusive brutality of a Christian Brother's education.

The second section, **Unmasked eyes in half-masked space**, borrows its title from Ezra Pound's *Pisan Cantos*, written during his imprisonment by the Allies after World War II in a cage overlooking Pisa. It reflects on the moment of insight when understanding comes despite impediments. These articles explore the reforming of juvenile justice, the management of disaster recovery, the establishment child protection services, reforming intellectual disability services, navigating the turbulence of the Kennett years in healthcare, the amalgamation of Albury-Wodonga's health services, and the establishment of Nurse Practitioners in Victoria.

The title of the third section, **Builder not sacker**, is derived from Seamus Heaney's poem *Dansom*, where a bricklayer, assailed by ghosts of the past finds strength in his craft. This section is more reflective, considering themes of care and compassion in mental health services, rural health infrastructure, the future of hospitals, the impact of rights-based legislation on disability care, changes in social administration such as privatisation and consumer-directed care, child-centred approaches to education, and the inadequate response of major political parties to regional health needs.

The fourth section, **Alphonso watched the door**, references a poem by Gerard Manley Hopkins that celebrates the mundane as significant. For me, bemusement at the inane ambitions of our politicians, learning from and celebrating my Irish heritage and importantly, the joys of poetry and song.

The final section begins, a little tongue-in-cheek, with a quote from Ben Jonson's **On my Picture Left in Scotland,** in which the poet wonders if, however eloquent he is, he will be taken seriously in his old age. In it I discuss where I think the past fifty years our experience has left us, and perhaps, what is to be done.

All infelicities of style and errors of fact or omission are mine alone, though I believe that any mistakes have been honestly made.

Section 1: *In my beginning is my end*

In my beginning is my end. In succession
Houses rise and fall, crumble, are extended,
Are removed, destroyed, restored, or in their place
Is an open field, or a factory, or a by-pass.
Old stone to new building, old timber to new fires,
Old fires to ashes, and ashes to the earth
Which is already flesh, fur and faeces,
Bone of man and beast, cornstalk and leaf
T.S. Eliot from East Coker, Four Quartets

1

Broady Boy

Broadmeadows in the 1960s and early 70s was more than a suburb; it was a microcosm of post-war Australia, grappling with rapid change and cultural integration. Situated about 10 kilometres north of Melbourne's CBD, Broadmeadows was then the city's northwestern frontier, known for its struggles with poverty, community unrest, and violence.

After World War II, Melbourne's population surged as soldiers returned and started families. Concurrently, Australia launched a significant post-war immigration drive, inviting families from Europe, particularly the United Kingdom, to settle for a nominal fee. They were known as the "ten pound poms." Or as Eric Bogle describes himself, the "Ten Quid Tourists". This immigration wave, aimed at bolstering the nation's defence and economy, led to the development of extensive public housing estates on Melbourne's fringes to accommodate the growing workforce needed for newly established manufacturing industries. The result was two wide arcs of public housing and industrial activity; one in the northwest that extended from west Heidelberg, through Broadmeadows to Sunshine, and the other in the southeast that ran from Frankston to Noble Park and Dandenong.

Children and young people were everywhere. The local Catholic parish school, Corpus Christi, had more than 1,000 students. Our third grade comprised three classes, each with over 70 students, housed in an aging building with a retractable wall. One class was held on its enclosed veranda. On Sundays, the building served as the parish church, until the local families managed to raise enough funds to construct the world's ugliest church (scale preferenced over aesthetics) on Widford Street, opposite the school. During lunch breaks, waves of boys played "British Bulldog," with each round pulling more participants into the centre until the massed group downed a final, daring child. Others played marbles ("alleys") in the mounds of earth that dotted the still-unpaved schoolyard or chucked yonies (small stones) or brinnies (large stones) at one another. The nuns were gentle, caring, and fierce. If you were caught outside your designated play area you could find yourself waiting outside the principal Sr Andrew's office for a switch of the cane on the back of your legs. They must also have been accomplished teachers because from those crowded classrooms came lawyers, teachers and academics as well as more than a few larrikins. The parish church had three packed masses on a Sunday morning, extended to another on Saturday evening and on Sunday afternoon when the communion fast was reduced from overnight to three hours.

In Broadmeadows, the housing estates formed a vast, working-class community. Street life in Broady during the 60s and early 70s, was dominated by 'sharpies'. Sharpies were a Melbourne creation, a product of an excess of young people with an excess of time on their hands. Then, as in most other times, young people wanted to spend time with their mates. With televisions still sparse, very often time was spent in the strip shopping centres. Sharpie style was distinctive and embraced its working class origins. Sharps borrowed something from the UK Bover Boys, but without the existential angst. I never saw NF (No Future) graffitied on walls. Their hair was generally short at the front and unkempt at the back, a precursor to the mullet, and in contrast to the mop-topped "mods" whom they despised. Their most distinctive clothing was high waisted pants and the striped cotton knitwear, the "connie" that was made by Mr Conti in Thornbury. At a high end, sharpie clothing included pin stripped suits and platform shoes, though these were not common in Broady. Their music was AC/DC and Lobby Lloyd, the Stones rather than the Beatles. The girls, or "brushes", wore jeans or denim mini-skirts and the chunkiest shoes they could find, often with cork bases, or "treads", shoes with a sole made from old tyres.

The sharpie groups, ("gangs" seems too pretentious a description) defined the social order in Broadmeadows in the 1960s. The JA boys, ANA boys, Olsen Place boys, and King Street boys marked territories that they controlled, enforcing unwritten rules about movement and association. Each had a designated area that they controlled and there were rules about where you went outside your area particularly on a Friday or Saturday night. Breaking the "rules" meant harassment and sometimes a beating. If you were associated with respected families, you could get a leave pass and could usually go unbothered. This meant that I got fewer blood noses than most. For the most part however, these groups maintained a predictable, albeit rough, equilibrium, with skirmishes often staged as formal confrontations.

Growing up in this environment meant navigating a landscape where affiliations could offer protection or peril. While violence was a constant threat, there was a semblance of order and community. Some, like the Glasgow families who lived around Olsen Place, exemplified the toughness and resilience that defined the area. Yet, within this hardened exterior lay pockets of warmth and care, especially from the matriarchs who looked out for the younger generation. Mrs C, the tough as nails matriarch of one the hardest of the Glasgow clans was always solicitous of my health. I was the probation officer of some of her sons, but she saw me as a local who understood how things were done and who in the end wanted the best for her boys.

Every now and then there would be sorties outside the area for confrontations with the Reservoir or Preston boys. It became really dangerous however in the late 60s when the younger brothers of "the boys" grew to an age when they wanted to emulate or exceed their older brothers. They did not respect the rules and could be particularly vicious. My brother Dan got a savage beating once and I spent a night in Royal Melbourne Emergency Department when I refused to let a pissed sharpie group invade a youth club I was running. There was some compensation when a local priest invited me to join him in a visit to the leader of that group's home, lifted him shoulder height with one arm, laid him across the bonnet of a car and invited him to reconsider his life choices. At one stage the JA boys tried to extend their reach into ANA territory and all-out war briefly broke out. The once prosperous and vibrant Justin Avenue (JA) shopping strip became a burnt out and boarded up wasteland with no traders.

As Broadmeadows evolved, the arrival of new migrant communities from Turkey and the former Yugoslavia in the 1970s brought additional layers of complexity. These groups introduced different cultural tensions, with historical enmities sometimes playing out in the local soccer fields, further fraying the already strained social fabric. The once relatively simple territorial disputes of the sharpies were overshadowed by deeper, more passionate conflicts rooted in old world rivalries.

In the end young people grew up; some found jobs and families, some stayed on the streets, and some became career criminals. Shane C became one of Victoria's most dangerous hard men. Peter, who knocked out my front tooth in the schoolyard in primary school, was murdered and dismembered in a falling out amongst drug dealers a few years ago. For those young people whose life style and family circumstances led them into illegal activity, life was bleak. Youth detention centres could be brutal, and they were exposed to a violence that was often sexual in nature. They learned to impose themselves on others and to trade sexual favours for survival. Often the police with whom they dealt were also brutal. Olsen Place Police Station and Northcote Crime Cars were the worst. If taken there the boys invariably took a beating and confessed to a string of offences that helped clear the police books. In Brunswick and Broadmeadows I worked with many young people who lived life with an immediacy and an intensity. Many of them sorted out their lives and moved on. Some became hardened criminals and more than a few, had short lives.

Sharpie culture came to an end in part because the territoriality that distinguished it became no longer relevant, and the social context became more diverse. Supermarkets destroyed the strip shopping centres. More young people stayed in school and work was not limited to Broadmeadow's factories. Drugs became a factor that did not recognise suburban boundaries. As drugs became more prevalent, young people travelled to obtain them and to socialise. The insular character of Broady and its sharpie neighbourhoods disappeared.

In the end, Broadmeadows' story is one of transformation; a suburb that mirrored the broader narratives of post-war Australia, from its struggles with poverty and assimilation to the eventual dispersal of its tight knit, if turbulent, communities. The fading of the sharpie culture marked the end of an era, leaving behind lessons on resilience, adaptability, and the enduring quest for identity in a changing world.

2

My Father's Hat

My father's hat was ubiquitous. It went where he went. He was forever looking to find where he had put it when he was going out or when he was leaving to come home. It wasn't a stylish hat. It was a working man's hat of the sort worn by many men of his generation; particularly those who came off the land where exposure to the elements was a daily hazard.

Allan Edward Keating, my father, was born in July 1921 – less than three years after the end of the Great War. He was born into a farming family, which had selected land in each generation from the 1840s under Victoria's successive land Acts; a rich history that he himself documented later in his life. His parents, Dave and Doris (Wade) Keating followed that tradition and moved from the family home in Quambatook to select land at Patchywollock in Victoria's far North West. They had 11 children, two of whom died as infants and one who did not survive childhood. Doris was a teacher, and she set up local schools twice in her own house and then in a corner of their property. Though my father left school after the Merit Certificate (about the equivalent to year 8) his mother instilled in him a love of knowledge and fostered the inquiring mind for which he was known.

The Keating family came from Ardfinnan, near Clonmel in South Tipperary, Ireland. My mother's people, I understand, came from Clare, and so it is not surprising that they chose to settle in the coastal wind swept area around Warrnambool. My father's people chose the open broad acre farming areas of the Mallee, which is consonant with the place from which they came. I have always been struck by the continuity between the character of people and the place in which they live. My father's people were open hearted, warm, and generous, in keeping with the land from which they came and where they chose to settle. My father loved the Mallee, and his heart never left it.

Tragedy struck the family with the death of a brother, Jack in early adolescence and Doris died in 1932 of acute peritonitis. The family lost the farm in the economic depression that gripped the world in the early thirties. Dave Keating moved his young family back to Quambatook, the place my father would always consider home. He always talked with great affection about his adolescence spent in Quamby. One day on his way from school, he was stopped by Mr. Fred Darcy, the owner of the general Store, who offered him a job. That was the beginning of a lifelong friendship with the Darcy family, and the beginning of his career as a bookkeeper. He developed outstanding skills in keeping accounts. Many years later when I was in school, he would bring from his work huge wads of accounts with long lists of figures on them. He would run his finger quickly down the lists of figures and tally them. He would then throw the piles to me and ask me to check them using a mechanical adding machine. I cannot recall ever finding an error in his totals.

My father signed up for the Army in 1939 and was quickly shipped to North Africa. He was not one of the originals in the 2/23 Battalion, 9th Division, that fought Rommel in Tobruk, but he joined them soon after, fighting at El Alamein, the turning point in the war in North Africa. His service record is a roll call of the most significant battles fought by Australians in the war; Alamein, Lea, Milne Bay, Finschhafen and Tarakan. He was famously the last man off Borneo in 1945 and turned the lights off in the GHQ. He rose in rank to become a Staff Sergeant, turning down a commission as a Warrant Officer, because he thought the promotion should go to another man who was older and who had seen longer service than him. He made many great friendships during the war, and he also lost good friends.

**Sgt Allan Keating, 2nd/23rd Division,
9th Div. AIF, aged 18yrs, 1939.**

After the War, Allan Keating returned to Quambatook and then worked in different places in rural Victoria before meeting and marrying Agnes Burk in Warrnambool in 1952. They eventually found their way to Melbourne, where Allan took out a war service loan to build our family home. He had always hoped that he would inherit the farm at Quambatook, but his great uncle, Chicken, inherited it from his brother, married late in life and sold it up. Allan was never to get back to the Mallee except to visit.

Where we lived in Melbourne was the outer suburbs in the late 50s and early 60s. At first the roads weren't built, and the area was not sewered. The Church, Corpus Christi Parish, was the centre of community life, and a good part of our lives revolved around an enclosed Catholic community. My father played a role in this community, but always an unassuming one. Others were prominent and received praise and recognition for their contributions. My father was quietly out the back counting the Sunday collection or pounding the pavement doing the parish census. Or he would get me to go with him on a Sunday afternoon to push the lawnmower down to the church and mow the lawns when no one else was around.

Allan Keating was a gentle man. I don't believe that he ever knowingly did harm to another person and he seldom if ever raised his voice. He wasn't a garrulous person, he was not a great talker, but he communicated his care for his family in simple and genuine ways. The best memories I have of my childhood are of going to the football every other week with him, and a few family friends; of traveling by train to Victoria Park to see Teddy Fordham kick ten goals and Essendon thrash Collingwood; and of sleeping in the old wooden stand at Windy Hill overnight to get finals tickets. He doted on my sister Mary and accompanied my sister Cathy every week, summer or winter, to athletics. I never saw him happier than when she won the Victorian Junior Cross Country Championship.

Dad was an old time Labor man, of the Curtin/Chifley variety but when the split came in 1956, he let his allegiance slip. If it came to a choice between his Party and his Church, there could be no contest. In his later life he warmed to the Hawke/Keating Labor Party, seeing in it some of what he admired from a earlier time.

Allan Keating was wary of alcohol. His own father was often affected by drink in his old age and dad himself worried after he came back from the war, that he could also. He had a beer as an appetiser before his Saturday evening meal and occasionally with old friends at the RSL, but this was very seldom.

He was a good man. Had God sometime decided that he had had enough of us and would send an avenging angel to destroy this world for its wickedness but would desist if he could find only one just man, Allan Keating would have been your man. He was my moral compass. I knew what was right, because he knew what was right. He was a constant man. We knew that whatever we did he would always be there, constant in his support. While he had views about what we did, he let us make our own mistakes and was there to back us up when we needed it.

Allan Keating was also the rock of his extended family. He was the one that everyone came to for advice or assistance. His was a calm and rational council. It was a role he played throughout his life.

Allan Keating was a man of simple but deep faith. I have a vision of him as I looked along the long hallway at home, kneeling beside his bed in prayer.

His great passion in later life was historical research. He published four books, one on family history, and another on the settlement of the eastern Mallee, a third containing his reflections on the war, and another with John Nolan on the Coughlan family. He also prepared a detailed roll of all those who served in the 2/23rd Battalion, including the theatres of war in which they served. This was an extraordinarily meticulous piece of research, and one for which many former battalion members and their families will be forever grateful. He did not have the education to be a particularly skilled writer but what he lacked in literary skills, he made up with meticulous research.

My father's hat is emblematic for me. No nonsense, utilitarian and unpretentious like the man. Beneath that working man's exterior however was the kindest, most patient and most generous of men.

3

Snowdon's Guilty Secret[1]

The dark centre of Joseph Heller's great comic novel, Catch-22, is Snowdon's guilty secret. This was captured in Mike Nichols 1970 screen adaptation, in a scene which recurs throughout. Yossarian, the novel's anti-hero, has worked to staunch the bleeding from the tail gunner's wounded leg, and cannot understand why Snowdon, apparently ok in his flight suit, lies still and claims to be cold. He finally unzips the flight suit and the airman's insides tumble out. Snowdon's guilty secret is that within the suit, he is shot away. The scene picks up the central themes of the novel, the iconic title; *Catch-22*, that you are damned if you do and damned if you don't; that things are not what they seem, and for Yossarian, the lesson that vitality is all – anything is justified that leads to survival.

For the many who suffered abuse by the Christian Brothers at St Joseph's Junior College in Pascoe Vale, Snowdon's guilty secret is a motif also for their experiences; things are not what they seem, pain must be hidden and disguised, and to survive is sometimes the best you can hope for.

St Joseph's school was established in 1956 as a feeder school to St Joseph's Christian Brother's College in North Melbourne. This was the height of the baby boom period, when the primary schools in Melbourne's expanding northern suburbs were exploding. The school was established in the middle class enclave of Pascoe Vale South at the end of the West Coburg tram line, a socio-economic world away from the northern working class suburbs

---

1. Published in Broken Rites 2004.

that surrounded it. The Brothers promised here, and in their other similar junior school in Essendon, a more select education than was available in the overcrowded parish primary schools.

In the late 1960s, the benign Br Hayes, was replaced as principle by an authoritarian moral conservative, Br Keith Weston. We knew him as Tex. He was an evil man. Weston was tall and meticulous with a pungency about him from the overpowering aftershave that he wore. He was much admired by the parents of the school, as an authoritarian. He stood for "standards" by which was meant social and moral conservatism and conformity. The distaste that many of us have come to have for the hypocritical Right has been fed by the conflict that we observed as children between these "values" and the corruption of their promoters. Weston would prowl the schoolyard punishing misdemeanours brutally with the strap he carried up his sleeve. Having unpolished or scuffed shoes was sufficient cause for a beating. This same guardian of conservative values was also sexually abusing many boys in the school.

Weston's mode of operation was consistent. He targeted young boys in early pubescence, at a time of maximum personal and sexual vulnerability. He would approach them in the schoolyard or corner them in hallways after school. On occasions he would summon them from class. Under the guise of counselling them about puberty, he would sexually assault them. He would insinuate that family members or friends were complicit in the abuse, swear them to secrecy and attempt to groom them for further abuse. And there was an element of class exploitation in his actions. He targeted those children from devout working class families beyond the immediate middle class environs of the school; those who were most in awe of the religious and who saw access to this education as a means of achieving a better life for their sons. They were grateful for what they believed they were being given. They were more trusting, less likely to ask questions and their children knew, unlikely to believe allegations of wrongdoing by the brothers. Many of the more than twenty known victims of Weston grew up within a half mile of one another, but did not speak to each other about their abuse.

It is hard to explain how it can come to pass that nothing is said, though it is still the case that many children today suffer in silence. Religious schools were different then, however. The Brothers were all powerful and considered as saints by the parents of the school. The holy Brothers and Nuns! Our children, mercifully, are more outspoken and independent. They would not stand for personal infringements, and we are more aware of the possibilities of abuse of power. The shame was internalised. There was something wrong with the victims that this had happened to them. It was their guilty secret that if people knew, would cause them to see how fundamentally bad they were. Most have been only able to speak to those closest to them in recent years, and at a time when the consuming tasks of child rearing and career building have no longer been available to block out their pain.

We were taught at Pascoe Vale by a succession of sadists, psychopaths and fools. Weston was the worst but was not alone. Brother D in year six beat us unmercifully for minor transgressions, usually involving failures in rote learning. On one occasion he strapped the whole class for errors and then proceeded to hear the same lessons again and again without opportunity for revision, with further beatings after each examination. Old Brother M in year seven promoted a cult of personality and commitment to himself while espousing anti-Vatican II theological and political drivel. Brother S in year ten attempted to engage at a more intelligent level but could not resist adopting a menacing and bullying attitude. Most of the brothers appeared to need the adulation of young boys for their physical prowess and sporting ability. This was a perverse and menacing culture, with strong sexual undertones. Marian idolatry was rife. "No child of Mary was ever lost" Brother M would quote Bernard of Clairvaux. But this masked an underlying misogyny. "Virgin most Pure. Virgin undefiled", we intoned in the daily litany, with the unspoken assumption that a woman who engaged in normal sexual relations was somehow unclean. And the culture could not tolerate difference. I met a good friend many years later when we were both well advanced in our university careers. He told me that he was gay, and despite his being one of the most outstandingly bright students in our year, he recounted that every day of his school life was one of intense anxiety and pain. I am ashamed that he was my friend, and I was not even aware of his pain.

Not all the brothers were like this. There were others, mainly at the senior college in North Melbourne, including Brothers Feehan, Wright and Dowsing, who were entirely admirable. They were distinguished by an ability to relate to young men with respect and as individuals in their own right. Brother George Frances the Principle at CBC North Melbourne was an extraordinary educationalist and inspirational leader. But their decency could not undo the depravity and heartlessness of their confreres.

We know now the clinical impact of post-traumatic stress, anxiety, depression, attachment disorders, sleep disturbance and relived experience. And we have become inured to tales of clerical abuse. But to truly comprehend the experiences of these boys, their story needs to be personalised. We need to think how it might be for your ten year old son to go off to school each day, and for that boy not to know if he will be beaten or abused by grown men, and that he will feel able to tell no-one. We need to understand that he may be scarred for the rest of his life by an inescapable sense of personal worthlessness, guilt and shame, however undeserved. That he will periodically experience such intense anxiety that it feels that every nerve in his body could explode, or that he may be unable to breathe, and this will give way to a depression and hopelessness so profound that he can see no future. Worst of all, that he will periodically lie awake all night and relive over and over again the invasion of his person, not as recurring memories, but as explicit felt experiences. He will have the smell of the obnoxious after-shave in his nostrils and feel the predator's hands on him. And that his family, spouse and children, will not understand the periodic withdrawal and inability to communicate, or an excessive consumption of alcohol, or an obsession with work as an escape from internal pain.

St Joseph's CBC Pascoe Vale Sth where dozens of young boys were sexually assaulted.

These were the experiences of those assaulted by Keith Weston, recounted with extraordinary consistency by men who had not previously met or who had not seen each other for more than thirty years. They had each been affected differently. Some have had lives of addiction and public pain. Many have had failed relationships. One attempted the religious life but could not deal with his feelings of personal unworthiness. At least one has taken his life. For the most part, they have remained silent into early middle age; on the surface, successful teachers, professionals and family men. They have kept the flight suit tightly zipped, worried that should they release the clasp, like Snowdon, their insides would come tumbling out.

Weston was finally brought to account for his crimes, but not before resisting for four years extradition from Queensland. When the untiring efforts of a courageous policeman, Det Stuart Delbridge were finally successful and he faced Court in October 2004, he sought to avoid prosecution because of ill health and beginning dementia. When this was rejected by Justice Stott, he pleaded guilty to a reduced number of cases, which would be below the threshold that allowed a lesser sentence. In the event he received a two and a half year suspended sentence. On the day of his trial, he was confronted at the Court by our friend Geoff's father, who faced him with the accusation "you killed my son". Those who have been able to retain some semblance of faith believe that he is soon to face a sterner judge.[2]

The Catholic Church, including the Religious Orders such as the Christian Brothers established a process to deal with cases of abuse by clergy. It was called *Towards Healing*. It was a farce. Claimants had few rights as the elapse of time and the ambiguity of the legal status of Religious Orders make civil suit a difficult course of action and so a very limited lever on responsiveness. Commitments for timely responses are rarely met, increasing the stress upon those who have taken the difficult step of confronting those they hold responsible for lives of suffering, and the low level of financial compensation eventually offered, demeaned the lived experience of the victims.

---

2. Weston died in 2011 on the night before he was to be charged with 13 further offences.

The core of the process was a mediation in which the harms were acknowledged, but the acknowledgement was partial and evasive. The process commenced with the silver-haired, silver-tongued spokesperson for the brothers giving an extended lecture to the victim about how different things are now, and that we need to understand that social norms were different forty years ago. As if it has ever been acceptable to beat and sexually abuse young children! The Brothers will accept that individuals will have done harm but would not acknowledge their collective failure to have provided a safe and ethical educational system, and that they are responsible for its failures. However well-intentioned they may now be, until they can own their responsibility, can say, "we did this", no vulnerable person can feel safe in their care. They have their guilty secret also. Clothed in the protective flight suit of remorse and reformed practice, they disguise a deep corruptedness.

In the case of Weston, their responsibility runs deeper. There is good reason to believe that his abuses were known but that he was moved from place to place to carry on his assaults. When he was confronted with his crimes, he was supported by the brothers to live in Queensland, out of the reach of the Victorian Courts and provided with legal assistance to avoid his accusers. The failure of the Order to require one of its members to act in an ethical manner and to assist him to avoid doing so increases its culpability.

Things are not what they seem. The abuse of individuals, the exploitation of a vulnerable class, and the diminished responsiveness to the victims of abuse are expressions of the wider Catholic Church's guilty secret – the abuse of power. The Church in Australia went through a revolution in the 1960s and into the 70s as a consequence of the Second Vatican Council. A central tenet of the Council was that the community of believers, not the hierarchy, constituted the church. The unaccountable authoritarianism of the magisterium was undermined by a greater openness and an engagement of non-clerics. This was a time of hope in which it was possible that the Catholic Church might become more human and less dogmatic.

But it did not take long for the Empire to strike back. John Paul II, that great champion of liberation in Eastern Europe, was the social and moral re-enslaver of the church. Under his leadership, and that of his chosen representative in Australia, Cardinal George Pell, theological dissent has been quashed, women marginalised, social and liturgical conservatism espoused, and clerical triumphalism reasserted. George Pell had been want to say that Australian Catholics are ungodly. They are not ungodly, but they are betrayed. The new disposition causes unease to the victims of abuse from another era. Beneath the appearances of an intact and healthy religious organisation which espouses moral conservativism, is a body shot through with the potential for abuse. This is not to suggest that the current hierarchy is involved in the abuse of children, but to recognise that abuse occurs where power imbalances are greatest, transparency denied, and accountability constrained.

In Catch-22, Yossarian has two responses to the dying Snowdon. The first is of humane if impotent comfort. "There, there" he says. What can you do for the lost but offer solace? The second is to challenge the inverted logic and hypocrisy of the war. *Catch-22* is a confrontation of inverted logic, where the insane is normal, the ill, healthy and death and disaster are given an acceptable face. For the victims of childhood abuse, there is far too much of the first of these responses, and far too little of the second. Some healing of those who have suffered all their lives is possible, if difficult and all our comfort need not be impotent. But it is the convoluted logic that allows the displacement of the deeply human by the appearance of moral virtue and social authoritarianism, that perpetuates the abuse.

4

Stalwart
(for Brian Venville)

Straight backed, unbending
you walked before us. You, me, and the mouse.
We hiked through forests.
Anywhere there was a train station to start and another
to take us home.

You took the heaviest pack,
weighted for size and strength.
We carried a canvass tent,
not light and compact but
of those our fathers used in New Guinea.
Cut spars from the bush and lashed with knots
I can still tie today.

We left a soft footprint; took out
what we took in.
Buried fireplaces as we left.
Only cut dead wood.

I see your broad back and heavy load before me,
single paced, unwavering.
I never saw you stumble.
But we each carried another weight,
not knowing the other's burden.
We carry it still.
You, now gravel voiced like your father.
Stalwart, still.

TP Keating (2025)

5

Pallotti College Millgrove

Pallotti College was built in the 1960s by the Pallottine Order of priests and brothers as a seminary. At the time, it was expected that many young men would enter religious life. The College was a large red brick building, designed in the shape of a cross, nestled into the hillside of Mount Ben Cairn in the Yarra Valley Ranges near Millgrove, just a few kilometres from Warburton. However, with the arrival of Vatican II and the changing times, the expected influx of vocations never eventuated.

Despite this, the College continued to operate, training a smaller number of clerical students, hosting retreats for parishes and religious groups, and serving as a base for youth camps. These camps were first established by Fr Gerhard Christoph and later continued by Fr Pat Jackson when Fr Christoph was transferred to Tardun in Western Australia.

The Pallottine Order was founded by St Vincent Pallotti in Italy in the mid-19th century, with a particular focus on engaging laypeople in the work of the Church. Officially known as the Society of the Catholic Apostolate, the order's presence in Australia was initially part of its German province. As a result, the Pallottines who arrived in Australia in the early 20th century were predominantly German. They were given responsibility for the Catholic missions in Western Australia, while the Missionaries of the Sacred Heart (MSC) oversaw those in the Northern Territory.

One of the Pallottines I was close to was Brother Joseph, an elderly German brother who had arrived on the northwest coast of Western Australia in 1912 with only a mandolin, a gift from his parents. Whenever I visited Millgrove, he would seek me out so we could play music together. Many of the German priests had lived through Nazi rule as young men, and some were forced into military service. Some carried deep emotional scars from these experiences. Some, like Fr Walter Sylvester were larger than life characters who were much respected in religious circles in Melbourne.

As a teenager, I attended school holiday camps at Pallotti College. In my mid-adolescence, Pat invited me to join his team, training youth leaders to work with young people across Melbourne. I worked with him for many years, training dozens of youth leaders who primarily served parish communities across Victoria. It was through this work that I met some of my most valued friends, including Frank Monagle and Shane (Sid) Ellis. The work was demanding but also exhilarating. We felt we were part of something meaningful, while also enjoying ourselves and learning skills that we carried back to our own community youth work. In many ways, I grew up with the Pallottines. The experience helped shaped my career, influencing my later work on the streets with young people and, ultimately, my decision between an academic career and working directly with people.

I was drawn to the social mission of the Pallottines. In the 1960s, Fr Jim Armstrong and Fr George Malina pioneered outreach to drug users on the streets of Melbourne. Fr Peter Willis and Fr Ray Hevern worked to support Indigenous communities to develop autonomy and self-governance of the missions. (In contrast to Pallottine Bishop Jobst of Broome, who reportedly set fire to an airstrip to prevent officers from the Whitlam government's Department of Aboriginal Affairs from landing). Fr Christoph and Fr Pat worked with young people.

Pallotti College also became a place of refuge for me. The chapel was a sanctuary. Kneeling on the red flagstone floor I felt protected from the abuse I experienced at school and its lingering effects. This led me to join the Pallottines, but I was not able to stay. What had once been a source of comfort became a source of intense internal struggle with feelings of unworthiness tied to my past experiences. Still, I gained immensely from my time with some confreres and from the mentorship of Pat.

During my time at the seminary, my neighbour in the next room was Gerry Mulvale. He had come from Perth and was a shapeshifter. First, he was an exaggeratedly pious seminarian whom we called "the bishop", then, after ordination, he was a caricature of the hip, modern priest. We always knew he was strange, but we did not know he was a monster. As an assistant priest at Syndal, a Melbourne suburb, he was accused of sexually abusing multiple young people in the parish. He was convicted and gaoled for assaulting two young men, and one young woman, who had been abducted and raped by him, tragically took her own life after being bullied by the Church to withdraw her charges. I am ashamed to say that the order I once admired went to extreme lengths to protect him, even to the point of blaming a 16-year-old boy for 'seducing' him.

The Royal Commission into Institutional Child Abuse found that 7% of Pallottines had been known to have engaged in abusive behaviour. While much of this occurred in the Western Australian missions by lay missionaries, it also involved several priests whom I had once admired and believed to be among the 'good guys.'

Today, the Pallottines in Australia are few in number and mostly elderly. Pallotti College is no longer a seminary but is a retreat centre run by volunteers and the order's headquarters in Studley Park Rd, Kew, has been sold to fund compensation payments for survivors of abuse.

Fr Pat Jackson quietly continues his life of prayerful service.

Section 2: *Unmasked eyes in half-mask's space*

there came new subtlety of eyes into my tent,

whether of the spirit or hypostasis,
 but what the blindfold hides
or at carneval
 nor any pair showed anger
 Saw but the eyes and stance between the eyes,
colour, diastasis,
 careless or unaware it had not the
 whole tent's room
nor was place for the full *EidwV*
interpass, penetrate
 casting but shade beyond the other lights
 sky's clear
 night's sea
 green of the mountain pool
 shone from the unmasked eyes in half-mask's space.
 Ezra Pound from Canto LXXXI

6

Juvenile Justice Reform in Victoria[3]

I watched with some sadness the proceedings of the Royal Commission on Institutional Abuse as it dealt with allegations of abuse in Victoria's state run institutions. The case studies given were heart rending for anyone who worked within that system in the 1960s and 70s. At the time I was in my first job as a Youth Officer in the Social Welfare Department, taking young people out of Turana and Winlaton and working with them in the community.

The case studies given were not entirely a surprise. Life for most children in the system was brutal and unforgiving. What did come as a surprise was that some of the abuse came from very senior carers and managers.

It must have been particularly hard watching for those who were managing and trying desperately to reform the system at that time. These were the great reformers; Ian Cox, David Green, Ken Williams, Mike Olijnyk, Lloyd Owen, Jim Murray and others; the people who will always be my professional heroes.

The 1960s were the peak of the explosion of the baby-boom child population. Vast Housing Commission estates were constructed that stretched across the north-west of Melbourne from West Heidelberg to Sunshine and the South-East from Frankston to Dandenong. With the inner city high rise flats, they were places where families with meagre resources worked hard to create a better life. They also became places of concentrated disadvantage and inadequate services.

---

3. First published in Eureka Street

The social welfare system was unable to cope with the scale and complexity of demands. It developed large institutions, *Turana* for young men, *Baltara* for younger adolescent boys, *Winlaton* for girls and *Allambie* for babies and young children. The conditions were poor, the service model unsophisticated and focused largely upon containment, and the staff largely untrained.

Congregate and institutional arrangements militate against appropriate child development and safety. The individual needs of children become lost. Children and young people who have been exposed to trauma and neglect have heightened needs which require an individual response. Institutional arrangements rely upon structure and regimentation which discourage individual initiative and problem solving. Children develop a diminished capacity for independent action. Institutions have significant power imbalances. Where this is the case, child to child or staff member to child abuse will take place.

Closed systems encourage abuse and the suppression of information. In the mid '70s Turana still had a population of more than 300, most of whom were not on a custodial sentence. Most young people were taken into care as being "likely to lapse into a life of vice and Crime" or "exposed to moral danger". Children could be incarcerated "Returned Director's Orders" on the basis of a phone call, with no process of adjudication.

The reformers put in place deinstitutionalisation and diversion initiatives and systems redesign. Numbers were reduced by alternative programs; staff were required to attend at least six months training; placement planning became based upon the needs of the child and the grounds for incarceration were becoming more formalised and rigorous.

The most important change was the introduction of case planning which placed the child or young person in the context of their family and their community, through the Department's newly established Regional Centres. Previously planning took place by untrained youth officers who focused upon the child in isolation. This over-emphasised the responsibility of the young person to change their circumstances. So, as was told in one of the Royal Commission case studies, a young girl could attend triad groups week after week and be told that she was not taking responsibility for herself, while carers ignored the fact that she was being repeatedly raped by her father.

The reformers' management of change created the environment for the first Cain Government's rights based legislation. The *Mental Health Act,* the *Intellectually Disabled Persons Services Act* and the *Children and Young Persons Act (CYPA) which* were enacted at this time, were what criminologist Stan Cohen has described as "do less harm" rather than "do more good" legislation. They limited the reach of government action with respect to vulnerable people. The CYPA separated the jurisdictions of Juvenile Justice and Family Welfare such that a child could be contained only after due process and for an adjudicated reason.

By the mid-80s and through the 90s Victoria came to have the most progressive and effective juvenile justice system in the country and was a leader internationally, with low incarceration rates and low recidivism. Critical elements were strong rights based legislation which promoted diversion and limited incarceration, a regionalised, professional workforce and a treatment technology grounded in psycho-social case work rather than punishment or retribution.

Much has been lost in the intervening years. An hysterical response to a few abscondings, a review by a former Police Commissioner with a correctional rather than a rehabilitation focus and a shift in community expectations towards retribution have made positive outcomes more tenuous. Regional Juvenile Justice teams however continue to work with young people at risk and their families in the context of their communities.

7

After the Deluge – some reflections on more than twenty years of disaster management[4]

It has been my privilege to have been closely involved in the management of recovery from the three of the largest natural disasters to befall the State of Victoria in recent memory. In 1983 I was given the responsibility of managing the operational aspects of the State's recovery from the Ash Wednesday bushfires. In 1993, as regional Director of the Hume Region, I was responsible for managing recovery from the largest flooding disaster to have affected the State. In 2003, in a similar position, I was called upon to manage recover from the North Eastern, and largest component of the Alpine bushfires. There have been countless other events between these, of course, but they have represented seminal events in our understanding of the processes of recovery management.

Ash Wednesday

Ash Wednesday was the first and most significant disaster event to occur in Victoria (and indeed south-eastern Australia) in the post Cyclone Tracy era. It occurred almost ten years after Tracy, but the shadow of that earlier catastrophic event hung over its management. The experience of Ash Wednesday, and the difficulties in its management, were to shape much of what came afterwards in recovery management in Victoria. It was an event of enormous

---
4. First published in Croaky, 2003.

proportions in which 75 people died, 2200 homes were destroyed and over four thousand people were dislocated. 359,000 hectares were burned. It occurred immediately after a terrible drought and at the end of a long hot summer. It left a blackened scar on the landscape which turned to heartbreaking mire when the autumn and winter rains soon followed.

It was in social terms, in fact three, if not four events: a rural fire in the south-west of the State, a forest fire affecting rural and tourist communities on the Otway peninsular, and two urban fringe fires, one in the relatively affluent Macedon ranges, and the other, in the eastern suburban fringe and semi-rural villages of the Dandenong ranges. One of the important lessons that we learned at the time, was that the experiences that people have in disaster situations, varies extraordinarily depending on their prior circumstances, their resources, both personal and social. Each of these "communities" had very different experiences, and we had to learn over time to respond much more flexibly than we expected to that variability.

While the shadow of Cyclone Tracy hung over the administration of recovery following Ash Wednesday as the most significant mass emergency event in the memory of those responsible, it was a very different event. It occurred in a relatively isolated and relatively unpopulated part of the country. Its civil administration was directly accountable to the Commonwealth government. Its recovery management was dominated as was the Katrina disaster in the US, by the threat of a public health disaster – a potable water supply could not be guaranteed. The bulk of the (white) population was evacuated, and the majority never returned. Its circumstances called for a militarily led management, and this happened, under the leadership of Major General Stretton. But its lessons for recovery were not great (since the bulk of the population was removed) or were not well understood. Nevertheless, its assumptions of military-like command management techniques, and orderly phased transfer from response to recovery persisted.

The administration of recovery following Ash Wednesday was itself another disaster, though one from which much was learned. The conceptual underpinning was flawed. It was assumed that recovery was a discrete phase, which commenced following response. It was assumed that resources and activity could be directed at will. The State Disaster Welfare Plan allocated responsibility to agencies (for instance, the Seventh Day Adventist Church was to be responsible for housing) without any regard for capacity to deliver. Relationships between statutory agencies were poor or non-existent as were communications channels between agencies. A recently elected government was keen to be seen to be doing things but lacked a policy framework to guide its actions. It ended up making decisions on the run, often announcing new assistance measures on the steps of Parliament, immediately following Cabinet meetings. and before there was a mechanism in place to deliver on them. The administration was vested in a branch of the Premier's Department, with no administrative infrastructure or systems. Applications for assistance were taken with poor attention to basic identifying and contact information and filed chronologically rather than by location or name of applicant. By the time application numbers got to 4,000, there was no way a specific file could be located. Most significantly, it was assumed that this would be over quickly. The problem would be dealt with, and everyone would be able to go back to their normal job.

The framework for managing recovery from Ash Wednesday was put together on the Saturday following the fires. While it was constantly trying to catch up, that framework has formed the basis of the Victorian model of recovery management, which has subsequently been taught through EMA training courses and has become the standard model in Australia, and increasingly in other countries. It may sound pedestrian now when this sort of thinking has become incorporated into the way we think about disaster management, but at the time it was revolutionary and challenging for those in central organisations and command agencies. It took as its beginning point that effected people should have a powerful role in determining how recovery was managed; that local organisation should be established around local government as the key coordinative mechanism; and that the resources of the State and other agencies should be brought in behind local organisation, rather than supplanting it.

We learnt many other things through 1983, which have become essential aspects of how Victoria manages emergency recovery. We were able to persuade decision makers that recovery was not a phase, which followed response but was integrally related to and concurrent with it. Decisions made during response activities have major implications for the way people recover. We learnt that coordination needed to take place regionally and locally, and that the role of central management needed to be to support and resource local managers. We learnt that public assistance must be clearly codified, understood by all and not changed during the management of any event and that the goodwill of donors can be put at risk where the distribution of assistance is not seen as fair and reasonable. And we learnt that the way assistance is given must reinforce the capacity, independence and dignity of people affected. Giving bicycles to children at Christmas is a very bad idea however well intentioned. Making it possible for parents to give bicycles to their children is a good one. Rev. John Hill designed and implemented the first comprehensive outreach personal services program, which involved home visiting everyone affected. We put in place the first Community Development Officer program, which gave eyes and ears to recovery and arms and legs to local communities. By the end, while nobody was satisfied that what was done was good enough, recovery management in Victoria and Australia was irrevocably changed.

October '93 Floods

On the night of 3 October 1993 eight inches of rain fell in a four-hour period on the Black Range above Myrtleford. The resultant flood overwhelmed the Broken, the Goulburn and the Ovens and King systems. Overnight Benalla was flooded and twenty bridges over the Ovens and King and tributaries were destroyed. Over subsequent days, flood waters moved towards Wangaratta and Shepparton. Wangaratta was narrowly reprieved by its levies and Shepparton also escaped flooding, though at the expense of farmers and orchardists to the east and north. Approximately a fifth of the State and much of Hume Region was under water at some time. It was the fourth largest natural disaster by area and by lost resources, in the recorded history of the country.

A distinguishing feature of this event was its breadth and diversity. There were in fact seven separate disasters which varied according to topography, the economy and means of production of the area, and the speed with which the floodwaters hit. Benalla, which was flooded overnight, had a very different experience from that of Nathalia, whose farmers watched as the waters crept across the country but destroyed their pastures just as effectively. Their pastures were still under water eight weeks later. Euroa and Violet Towns disaster was a flash flood, which caused a large amount of damage in a short period. The Ovens Valley had a violent experience with great damage done to infrastructure and with some communities isolated for days. A distinguishing feature was the variable capacity and commitment of Local Authorities to dealing with the issues their people faced. Benalla was approached to establish a coordinating committee on the first morning it was possible to get into the town. It had the committee established and was actively managing recovery that evening. It took Shepparton two weeks to employ the community development officers for which funding was provided, and we never really felt that the city was in control.

A flood is a very particular sort of disaster event. Its impact is insidious and pervasive but lacks the visual persistence that enables those not immediately affected to comprehend. Floodwaters recede, and for many observers the problem is resolved. The images are not as terrifying as those of wildfire and once the water is gone, there is not a blackened scar on the landscape to remind the public of the disaster. But the impacts can be far reaching. The experience for many, particularly the elderly, during the '93 floods, was traumatic. The smell of the floodwaters stayed for many weeks after the waters subsided, as a continuing reinforcement of that trauma. Some of our experienced psychiatric staff compared the experience they had of dealing for up to twelve hours a day with extremely stressed people, with some of the most intensive work they had done in psychiatric institutions. For some, there was anger and frustration at the failure of those outside to appreciate the degree of their distress. During the Christmas following the floods, there were major bushfires, which threatened Sydney. In fact, a relatively small number of permanent residences were damaged and most of these were insured, but the public outpouring was substantial. For people in Benalla, theirs became the forgotten disaster.

Financial losses were significant. We distributed more than $7m in assistance as emergency grants, temporary living assistance and for replacement of essential items. We had over 150 staff in the field for three months to make this and personal support possible. But this of course did not come close to addressing the financial losses involved. Over time, the Benalla Recovery Committee transformed into the Benalla Flood Action Committee which battled for a number of years, with some success, with insurance companies to get reasonable outcomes for those effected. You could not then insure for flood at that time, and so the debate becomes whether the damage was in fact caused by floodwaters, by storm damage, or by overflow from municipal drains. For rural communities, the removal of subsidies for the replacement of fencing and the transport of stock and fodder became powerful symbols of their belief that government was only interested in those in cities and towns.

The flood disaster reinforced the importance of the role of community development officers. On this occasion, because of their number and distribution, we employed a person to work beside them to provide coordination, training and support, and also, to enable them to record and report on their experiences. These reports became an invaluable record of the learnings from the event. We found during this event however, a need for a resource which was not previously understood. On the weekend after the flood a massed public meeting at the steps of the Benalla Municipal Offices expressed extreme anger at what was seen as the failure of the Victoria Police to provide adequate warning, and the perceived preferential treatment of some with respect to warnings. Over the following week, approximately 80 neighbourhood meetings were conducted by trained debriefers, led by Rob Gordon, Ruth Wraith and John Hill, which enabled the communication of important information about the night of the floods, and to genuinely have their say and be heard about the things which were of concern to them. Local police, who had spoken about being alienated from the community, talked after the meetings of having been accepted again as community members. Following this, similar community meeting took place across the region.

The floods provided a significant logistical challenge for recovery, especially with respect to cleanup. Exhausted people immediately affected by the floods were in need of volunteer assistance to make good their properties, and the VFF was very good at facilitating this. But it was very unreliable for very good reasons. People had their own properties to tend and their own families to care for. The extent of the floods meant that volunteers needed to come from outside the region, often travelling for much of a day to get here. Frequently promised numbers did not arrive, frustrating the plans of organisers and property owners.

One of the other important lessons from the floods experience, was concerned with the capacity of people affected by disasters to process information. In Benalla, while there were three letter drops to all households in the first week, advising people about assistance available and what to do about flood affected carpets, many complained that they did not receive this information. It is not surprising that people who are traumatised do not read, and if they do, do not retain much of what they read. We need to become more sophisticated about the way we convey information, with an emphasis upon direct communication.

Finally, we witnessed with the '93 floods, some important changes in the structure of rural social organisation. We watched as people effected by the disaster sought solace and support not from the traditionally potent social networks, such as the churches, but from emergent networks, notably associated with producer organisations. The VFF, the Tobacco and Hops Growers Association, the United Dairy farmers of Victoria, provided some of the most useful and sought after advice and support for people effected.

Alpine Bushfires 2003

The Alpine bushfires were distinguished principally by the length of time that they burned. The fires were caused by lightning strikes which fired the tinder dry bushland, which had suffered the worst drought in one hundred years. The fires burned for eight weeks and destroyed 1.2m hectares. They required the deployment of large numbers of fire-fighters and support staff and did substantial damage to tourism and farming enterprises. One fire came within five kilometres of the major urban centre of Wodonga and many small villages surrounding Bright were repeatedly placed on high alert. The fires created significant public health risks associated with smoke inhalation and water quality.

One of the important aspects of this event from a recovery perspective was that it compounded the effects of one of the worst droughts that the State has experienced. The fires hit communities, which had had their resources, physical, emotional and financial, drained. This, probably more than any other factor, determined the extent to which individuals and communities were able to deal with the disaster experience.

This event saw the establishment for the first time of a formal regional coordination mechanism for recovery. This was based upon the standing Hume Regional Recovery Management Committee, which had hitherto had a planning and development role. Given an operational role, and augmented with additional members, it provided the basis of coordination throughout the life of the event and recovery. It included the three Local Government Authorities affected by the fires, as well as all the relevant government departments, statutory authorities and non-government agencies. It took a genuinely whole of government approach, dealing as much with natural resources, primary industry, economic development and infrastructure issues, as it did human services issues. This was one of the most remarkably successful aspects of the management of the disaster.

The event also saw the introduction of an extremely successful initiative by the Country Fire Authority. Throughout the period in which the fires were burning, and when many smaller communities were experiencing threat, the CFA conducted locally based briefings, which ensured that people knew exactly what was happening. What we learned from this is that information before the fact is a powerful recovery tool. One of the ways in which disaster events traumatise people is that they induce a feeling of powerlessness. People experience a sense of defencelessness in the face of the elements. Information in this instance is literally power. Provided with accurate information about what is happening and their choices, people feel more in control. We experienced lower levels of stress and continuing psychological trauma associated with this event than expected, despite the repeated crises that some communities experienced. I believe that the CFA initiative was at least partly responsible for this. The obverse of this was that there was some trauma experienced as a result of the fact that many people did not understand the changed approach being taken to fire management. Contemporary approaches place an emphasis upon preserving assets and life rather than adopting aggressive firefighting strategies. There was deep resentment in some communities, which persists to this day, that the fire services did not seek to extinguish fires that subsequently burnt farmland.

Timely decision making by government was a critical issue. There was a very rapid response to the stresses experienced particularly in the Alpine Shire as a result of reduced tourism, prompted by a well-organised and articulate business lobby. The complex issues of private and commercial risk as against public responsibility however, made it more difficult to resolve the important issues for farmers.

And the fires raised some very important issues for the protection and management of health systems. There were at times, difficulties in getting an appreciation of some of the public health hazards being dealt with. Also, at one point there were three hospitals, caring for mainly elderly people, in the path of fires. It was clear that there was not systems in place to manage evacuations and demand transfer between health providers, identify available bed capacity and manage personnel and skills requirements should this be necessary.

Benalla, October 1993 (image copyright
Watermark, Benalla Ensign)

8

Some Issues arising from disaster recovery management

There are some questions arising from these experiences of major disasters, particularly with respect to three areas; the construct of 'community' and its implications for social administration, the pre-eminence of public health concerns in all their guises, and the particular challenges associated with delivering joined-up or 'whole of government' responses.

Community

A consequence of adopting the Victorian model has been the reification of the concept of community. We talk of 'community management" and establish "community committees" to guide recovery. We talk and try to act as though there is entity out there that we might be dealing with in a meaningful way. We develop intervention strategies based upon bogus or outdated sociology, which argues that there, are abiding social connections, which are somehow sundered in the experience of disaster, and it is our task to restore them.

To question the primacy of 'community' is to risk being pilloried as lacking a responsible beginning point, but we need to understand that an unquestioning and unsophisticated application of the concept leads us into poor recovery and poor social administration practice. The assumption of community brings with it an assumption of homogeneity, an assumption that there is a community perspective that can be obtained if only we use the right method or have the right orientation. It leads to the assumption of some ideal social state that that can be created or restored. But social life is `more complex than that. The reality is that there are complex patterns of social interaction between individuals and groups, and that associations are formed across multiple and competing domains. People associate by location, by affiliation and by interest. And those associations change over time and by interest.

What we usually mean when we talk of community, is the community of the powerful. We look to those who are most often seen as representing the interests of the majority – the local government representatives, business people, ministers of religion. With the best of intentions, these people cannot represent the interests, the understandings and the aspirations of the diverse range of people who are affected by disasters. They do not understand, much less represent the unemployed koori young person, the elderly bed bound person or the single parent struggling in rented accommodation.

So, what can we usefully retain from our 'community' discourse? 'Community' is a shorthand and is a heuristic concept in the sense of inviting us to attend in a particular way. It is shorthand firstly for 'not government'. We understand that while government is able to do much, there is much that it cannot do. At least some of what it cannot do as well as less formal means of organising, is to respond to the particularity of local concerns. Government must aggregate in order to maintain public accountability and is inevitably big and cumbersome. Community is in this sense a shorthand for local, small scale and responsive, in a way that governments find it hard to be. But we mean something less negative also. In our use of the language of community we are wanting to assert at least two other things. We want to argue that people should be, or need to be, in charge of their own recovery. That the quality of decision making will be better where those who are affected by decisions are involved in taking them. We argue that people have a right to participate in critical decisions that impact them. Further, we are asserting that there is a therapeutic value in the processes of citizen participation; that the processes by which people are engaged in decision-making are part of the restorative processes of social relationships.

So where does this leave our commitment to community management of recovery? I would argue that we can retain the commitment to the local, the participatory and the therapeutic, without having to accept the muddled romanticism of the language of community. To do so however will require that we become more rigorous not just with language, but also in addressing the complexities that that language masks. We need to develop much more aggressively democratic approaches which engage the broader range of affected people and recognises the diversity of interests that are always present within collectives of people, including an understanding that people's interests and preferences will vary over time.

Public Health

Public Health as an approach and as a service response is one of the most overlooked and yet most vital aspects of disaster recovery. We need only to look at the situation in the areas affected by Cyclones Katrina and Rita to see the potential impact of a major public health threat. Polluted water breeds disease. Poor hygiene can be a greater cause of mortality and morbidity than an initial disaster event. In each of the events to which I have referred, there has been a significant public health threat which has been belatedly identified and which has provoked a reactive response. In the case of Ash Wednesday, this was a mental health threat. No one anticipated the length of time it would take to restore a degree of normalcy to people's lives, or the level of generalised stress that this would entail, particularly for children. In the case of the '93 floods, we picked up late, and from a dropped comment from the Municipal CEO that there was a break in the sewer line that threatened the Benalla water supply, and that the municipal environmental health officer was on leave. During the 2001 alpine bushfires, it took us more than a week to put in place effective health alerts and advice concerning the dangers of sustained exposure to smoke. The deposit of ash toxics within the watercourses brought to light the high level of unregulated drawing of water for private consumption from rivers and streams. It also posed a major problem for the supply of clean water to urban centres, with a number of water purification systems threatened, and Wangaratta City's system failing on one day.

Old Public Health is essentially about hazard identification and management. Disasters change the balance within the natural and human environment. That means that we need, as a matter of course, re-assess the threats to human health and wellbeing posed by the new circumstances. We do this in a reactive and idiosyncratic way. It would be my intention in the case of any future significant disaster event, to move my public health staff off line (to the degree that this is possible, given the possibility that actual public health threats may be experienced) and require them to undertake a comprehensive public health risk analysis. We cannot afford to be surprised by a major outbreak of disease amongst an already vulnerable or displaced population.

But public health methodologies go further than this. Public Health is not just about hazard identification, surveillance and risk mitigation. It also involves an analysis of populations and their vulnerabilities. These also will change in the context of a disaster. We know that some population cohorts are more vulnerable in the event of a disaster. We know that if we are faced with an influenza outbreak it will be the elderly and the very young who will be most vulnerable, and so we will put in place population based interventions which target our activities to them. Surely, we should apply the same methodology to other events. We learned, for instance, from the '93 floods that elderly people at home were particularly at risk. They were anxious about their personal possessions including memorabilia. They had less access that those more mobile to information and so were anxious about what they did not know. And they were more vulnerable following sudden moves. We put in place an approach, which we have extended to all major events, whereby we immediately double the level of home care support available to users of HACC services. We know that it is important to provide security, comfort and support, and that this will avoid many problems into the future.

In order to put in place, proactive population based interventions, which will enhance the capacity of people to deal with the impact of disaster events; we need to know those populations intimately. Again, this is a task of the comprehensive public health assessment to which I referred, in conjunction with Local Government, which has that sort of knowledge. In order to deliver on this, we need to develop the methodology for local area population heath analysis, and we also need to develop a flexible approach to resource deployment, which recognises potential threat to health and wellbeing, as well as actual events requiring intervention.

Managing Whole of Government Responses

The coordinated response in the North East to the Alpine bushfires demonstrates what can be achieved in coordinating at a regional level, the activities of statutory agencies, local government, and non-government bodies. There was an extraordinary level of good will, openness and an absence of territoriality, which meant that residents in the fire areas could be assured that agencies were working closely together and services and supports would be coordinated. It also demonstrates the limitations that exist, within a complex government environment, upon joined up activities.

A tension inevitably arose between the imperative to resolve issues in a timely manner, as locally as possible, and in a way that took into account the responsibilities of other agencies, and the functional responsibilities of individual organisations. The Secretary of the Department of Infrastructure, for instance, was clear that he was responsible for dealing with issues of water infrastructure and called a statewide forum of agencies to address these issues. He put in place, not unreasonable, statewide strategies to meet his responsibilities, but which did not take account of regional coordination requirements or structures. Other Departments, the more time that had passed since the disaster event, gradually started to put in place their own granting arrangements, again which bypassed the agreed coordination and administration arrangements. From a Local Government perspective, this was frustrating and time-wasting. They had invested energy in the regional arrangements in the belief that there might be one point of contact with the State government and that agencies would act in a coordinated way.

While many issues were effectively dealt with within the Regional Recovery Committee, in the end, the matters that were of greatest significance, were ones which required a policy response at a state level. The issues of subsidies for farm fencing, and the making good of fire breaks on private property were the most significant for local communities but were not amenable to local resolution. The length of time that it took to resolve these issues and the level of anger and frustration that this generated locally had important implications for other aspects of recovery.

This is not to say that all aspects of disaster recovery could or should be devolved or managed regionally through coordinative mechanisms. There are some matters which have policy and financial implications which will inevitably be dealt with centrally. The responsibilities of the Department of Human Services under the Emergency Management Act are concerned with the coordination of government activity and properly leave the functional responsibilities of other Departments intact. It is however to point out that there are tensions between the tendencies of agencies to line manage issues, and the requirement to coordinate activities between agencies, and the not unreasonable expectations of local and regional players that government will deliver a joined-up response to complex issues which effect communities in complex and interrelated ways.

There is, however, another and more serious way in which whole of government coordination is difficult and which has implications for the management of disasters. I give as an example the complexity of managing water. On one weekend (which in accordance with Murphy's Law happened to be a long weekend) a thick slurry which had been deposited in the Ovens River moved down to Wangaratta and caused the city's filtration system to fail. This was clearly a water supply problem, but it was also an environmental problem and a health problem. Who was responsible for managing the complex issues involved. Was it the water retailer? The Catchment Management Authority? The Environmental Protection Agency? Local Government? The Department of Human Services? The Department of Sustainability and Environment? or the Department of Infrastructure? The answer is all of the above.

Which issues took priority? It was not clear. Which agency, if any, was finally responsible? Again, it was unclear. In fact, the issue was managed very effectively. The water retailer, Goulburn Ovens Water, transported water from Benalla and restored the failed system. The collaborative arrangements which existed between agencies, and which were nurtured in the previous weeks of recovery management enabled an effective multi-agency response. But that need not have been the case, and in any place other than the north-east it probably would not have. The fact is that the business of government is complex. It involves multiple and complex responsibilities which overlap and compete. The same issue can be approached from multiple legitimate perspectives. We have done the easy stuff of joined up government. We have even done some of the hard stuff. We are now faced with some of the very hard stuff.

9

Protecting Victoria's Children

Child protection in Victoria has developed over more than a century, shaped by various social, political, and legal changes that reflect evolving attitudes toward children, families, and the state's role in family intervention. From the early child welfare practices of the 19th century to the modern child protection system, history shows shifting perceptions of childhood and the protection of vulnerable children, influenced by specific policy decisions at critical junctures.

In the 1800s, under the British colonial system, a basic framework for child welfare was established in Victoria, driven by growing concern for children's well-being in a rapidly industrialising society. Early child protection focused on managing child labour and the care of abandoned or orphaned children. The Victorian Society for the Prevention of Cruelty to Children (VSPCC), founded in 1897, was one of the first organised efforts to intervene in cases of child abuse and neglect. The gold rush in Victoria resulted, particularly in Melbourne, in significant wealth and led to substantial bequests to religious and charitable organisations, which established large children's homes mainly in Melbourne's eastern suburbs and around Geelong.

At this time, much of the focus was on the protection of children from physical harm, often within the context of a growing awareness of the dangers of industrialisation, such as poor working conditions and child exploitation. The Victorian government began taking a more active role in child welfare, particularly as the orphanages and institutions became crowded with children who had been abandoned or whose families were deemed unable to care for them.

By the early 20th century, the child protection system in Victoria began to evolve into a more structured and institutionalised form. The Children's Welfare Act of 1928, expanded the state's role in child welfare, establishing a formal system of child protection. Under this act, authorities were granted the power to remove children from their families if they were considered to be at risk of harm, although the focus remained on children living in poverty or orphaned by disease or death of parents. Institutional care was heavily relied upon, with many children placed in government-run orphanages

A significant turning point came in 1962 with the publication of "Battered Child Syndrome" by American paediatrician Henry Kempe and colleagues. This research highlighted the physical signs of child abuse and argued that severe injuries inconsistent with parental explanations should be treated as potential abuse cases. This study had a substantial international impact, resonating with doctors, child welfare advocates, and law enforcement officers in Australia.

The "battered child" movement developed in Victoria during the 1960s as a response to the growing recognition of physical child abuse. Influenced by international developments in the US and UK, where child protection laws and research into non-accidental injuries were advancing, Victoria began seeing child abuse as a serious social issue. Previously considered a private family matter, child abuse was now recognized for its long-term impact on children.

The rise in public awareness of child abuse in the 1960s and 70s led to the establishment of various child protection services in Victoria, including the Children's Court, which handled child abuse and neglect cases more sensitively. New laws facilitated removing children from abusive situations and prosecuting offenders. There was a growing belief in the importance of keeping children within their families whenever possible, shifting child welfare practices toward family preservation and supporting struggling families rather than removing children. However, institutional care remained a key element of the child protection system.

By the 1970s, Victoria Police had become more active in prosecuting non-accidental child injuries, focusing primarily on physical injury in response to medical diagnoses. There was limited understanding or institutional response to neglect, emotional, and sexual abuse. Domestic disputes were often not investigated or intervened, as the family home was considered sacrosanct. This approach changed under the leadership of Police Commissioners Christine Nixon and Ken Lay. Until 1975, Victoria Police had a separate women's policing division, with welfare-related work viewed as women's police duties, not "real policing."

In 1975, the Children's Protection Society (CPS) was established as an authorised intervenor in child protection, allowing CPS and Victoria Police to enter premises without a warrant, investigate, and remove children if necessary. However, the relationship between Victoria Police and CPS was strained, with differing views on appropriate responses and criticisms of CPS's capacity to provide timely and adequate responses. By the early 1980s, the Department of Community Welfare Services believed child protection should be a statutory function and exercised by the department, leading to CPS conceding authority in 1983 as its service struggled.

This transfer was led by Merredith Sussex, with the program overseen by senior officers. I was responsible for the program and subsequently Robin Clark took over from me and managed the program for most of the next two decades. The program emphasised that children were best cared for within their families, initially placing a six-month limit on departmental involvement. Despite this, the resources that were committed to family support were limited. The scale of demand was underestimated, and the program rapidly became industrialised with demands for additional staffing and improved conditions.

Initially, the child protection system operated under a "dual track" model, with both Victoria Police and the department authorised to intervene. Over time, it was accepted that protective intervention assessments were beyond the police skill set, moving to a "single track" system, where police intervened only in emergencies or potential crimes.

The Children and Young Persons Act 1986, arising from the Carney Review of Child and Youth Welfare, formalised child protection management. It separated family and juvenile justice divisions and defined grounds for care admission. The Act rejected a non-adversarial adjudication system such as that operating in

South Australia. That decision contributed to the lengthy case adjournments and prolonged uncertainty for children that has bedevilled the program ever since.

Having formally taken on the role, the department could no longer quarantine itself from public scrutiny when things went wrong, as they inevitably did. Periodically a case would come to public attention where a child had been seriously injured or killed. There would be very public scrutiny of actions taken and the department was ultimately responsible. External parties provided a critique of the department's actions. In particular, the social work department of the Royal Children's Hospital (RCH) was a strong advocate on behalf of children. The RCH advocated mandatory reporting, the legal requirement that nominated personnel from a variety of professions including teaching, nursing and child care, formally notify the department of any concerns with respect to the safety of a child. Robin and I both strongly opposed mandatory reporting. We argued that it misdescribed the child protection "problem" as one of case finding. In most cases however, children who were seriously injured or killed were well known to the care system. The fundamental "problem" was not case finding but of knowing how to intervene to make a difference.

The issue of mandatory reporting came to a head in 1986, associated with public concern about the care of a young child, Daniel Valerio. Daniel had been admitted to the emergency department of Frankston Hospital with unexplained physical injuries. He was attended by the Police Medical Examiner and released to go home. He was subsequently killed at home. There was a public outcry that this child had been killed and the department was under substantial pressure. The minister at the time sought advice from his Child Protection Advisory Committee of which there were two chairs. One chairperson, Delys Sargeant, a respected academic who was opposed to mandatory reporting was overseas at the time, the other, a federal court judge recommended that mandatory reporting be adopted, as was being advocated by the RCH and other interested parties. This was despite Daniel's case being well known to the care system and the fact that his release from hospital was authorised by the police medical examiner. The most profound change in the child protection system was driven not be evidence based policy making but to contain a political backlash.

The impact on the child protection system was dramatic. Protection notifications rose from about 3,000 per year to 30,000. The program staffing increased, and the child and family support aspects of the program were further dwarfed by the forensic component. From this point, child protection practice was irrevocably changed. No government would be able in the future to change the requirement for mandatory reporting for fear of being blamed for the next child tragedy.

As the program grew it became elaborated with risk frameworks and protocols. Robin said to me on one occasion that the staff were concerned that they had to take very serious decisions with little support. In response she introduced a protocol whereby significant decisions concerning a child's welfare and status would be signed off by a more senior practitioner. Over time this came to be seen by child protection staff as a lack of confidence in them and a bureaucratisation of the service. In 2001 while on sabbatical leave at Trinity College Dublin, I undertook a comparative review of the Victorian and Irish child protection systems. I found at that time that the Victorian system had a strong centre and a weak periphery, that is, it had a strong rules driven central function but had degraded the skills and capacities of frontline workers. The Irish system had a weak centre and a strong periphery. It had few central controls and supports but was skilled and capable at the point of delivery.

In 2004, I attempted at a regional level to introduce a no fault review system based upon public health root cause analysis models. This was in response to a strong centralising and blaming culture that had come to dominate the program, prioritising fault finding over learning. I argued that staff should be supported to identify difficulties and mistakes in managing cases and to learn from these in collaboration with their peers, rather than to hide them for fear of retribution. The centre quickly assumed control of the process however and restored a blame attribution ethos.

In 2004 the Secretary of the Human Services Department Patricia Faulkner, ordered a review of the child protection program. That review, undertaken by Alan Consulting identified that 60% of notifications to the department of suspected child abuse were re-notifications. This meant that the larger proportion of notifications were indeed well known to the care system, were being assessed as not requiring statutory intervention and were then discharged with little support until they were again notified. This review contributed to a further shift toward early intervention and the promotion of family support services. The *Victorian Child Protection Framework* of 2005 emphasised the importance of collaborative, multi-agency responses to child abuse and neglect, and prioritising family preservation wherever possible. While significant additional resources were provided to non-government organisations to provide family support, this continues however to be dwarfed by the resources that are committed to forensic child protection investigations.

In recent years, there has been growing focus on the over-representation of Aboriginal children in the child protection system, with the Victorian government acknowledging the legacy of colonisation and its impact on Aboriginal families. The *Commission for Children and Young People* was established to ensure that children's voices are heard in matters of policy, with particular attention to Indigenous children and families.

Over the four decades, that I have been closely involved with or have observed child protection, the state's role has expanded significantly. Initially having no role, the state wrestled control from CPS, only to struggle with the demands of forensic intervention. While many children have been removed from abusive situations and some have experienced improved circumstances, the system has been overwhelmed by forensic demands, often failing to provide adequate family support to prevent the need for statutory intervention.

10

Indigenous Participation in Child Protection in Australia: The Hume Aboriginal Family Decision-Making Program[5]

For decades, Aboriginal and Torres Strait Islander children have been significantly over-represented in Australia's child protection system. Despite comprising only a small percentage of the population, these children make up a disproportionately high number of cases within child welfare services. This is not a recent phenomenon but rather the continuation of a painful history of forced removals that have left lasting scars across generations. The policies that once sought to forcibly assimilate Aboriginal children into white society have evolved, but the legacy of these practices still looms large over Indigenous families today.

Throughout much of the 20th century, the government systematically removed Aboriginal children from their families under the guise of welfare. Special laws placed Aboriginal children under the guardianship of state-appointed protectors, overriding the rights of their parents. These removals were based not on proven cases of neglect, but on racial classification, with lighter-skinned Aboriginal children considered more likely to assimilate. Later, the removal of Indigenous children continued under general child welfare laws, which disproportionately impacted Aboriginal families, many of whom had limited access to social welfare support. The

---

5. Derived from a paper given at IPSCAN Congress, Berlin, August 2005. Subsequently, the Department transferred responsibility for Indigenous child protection to the Aboriginal Child Care Agency (ACCA).

effects of these policies are still felt today, with intergenerational trauma, socioeconomic disadvantage, and systemic discrimination contributing to the continued over-representation of Indigenous children in child protection and juvenile justice systems.

Understandably, Aboriginal communities have developed a deep distrust of state child welfare authorities. The forced separations of the past have left many Indigenous families wary of government intervention, and traditional case planning approaches have often failed to engage Aboriginal families in a meaningful way. In response, initiatives such as the Aboriginal Family Decision-Making Program (AFDM) have been developed as culturally appropriate alternatives to conventional child protection strategies. Operating in rural Victoria, AFDM aims to empower Indigenous families and communities by involving them in decision-making processes about the welfare of their children.

The AFDM program was developed as a collaboration between the Rumbalara Aboriginal Cooperative and the Department of Human Services. It was designed as a culturally safe, community-led approach that prioritised the involvement of Elders and extended family members in discussions about child protection. Rather than relying on government authorities to make unilateral decisions, this program ensured that Aboriginal families had a central role in planning for the care of their children. At its core, AFDM seeks to keep children within their communities and extended families, providing them with the cultural and emotional support they need while also ensuring their safety.

The philosophy behind family decision-making is that families, when given the right support and information, are better equipped than government agencies to determine what is best for their children. The program follows a model where meetings are conducted in a culturally respectful manner, with family members, community Elders, and agency representatives coming together to create child-centred, family-focused care plans. These meetings are held in places chosen by the family, allowing them to feel comfortable and engaged in the process. A key feature of the program is the use of private family time, where relatives can discuss options freely before presenting a plan to professionals for consideration.

Early evaluations of the program have been overwhelmingly positive. Families that participated in the AFDM program have seen significantly fewer cases of children being removed from their care. Before the program's introduction, many of these cases would have resulted in court orders and out-of-home placements, often with non-Indigenous carers. With the AFDM model in place, children are more likely to remain within their extended family network, avoiding the distress and disconnection that come with forced removal.

The success of AFDM has also led to increased trust between the Aboriginal community and child welfare authorities. For years, government agencies were seen as enforcers of separation, but through meaningful partnerships with Indigenous organisations, these relationships are beginning to change. The collaboration between the Department of Human Services and Aboriginal organisations is not just a symbolic gesture but a genuine attempt to share decision-making power. The program fosters an environment where responsibility is distributed between government agencies and Indigenous communities, reinforcing the idea that Aboriginal families have the right and the capacity to care for their own children.

Despite its success, the AFDM program faces several challenges. Ensuring adequate funding and resources remains a concern, as does the issue of balancing government oversight with community autonomy. Questions have been raised about whether the family decision-making process should only be initiated through child protection notifications or if it should be made available more broadly to support families before crises occur. There are also concerns about confidentiality and the responsibility of the state to ensure child safety, even when decision-making is shared with Indigenous communities. These issues require ongoing dialogue and refinement to ensure that the program continues to serve the best interests of Indigenous children.

The AFDM model in Shepparton has demonstrated that culturally informed, community-driven approaches can improve outcomes for Aboriginal children in child protection. However, the lessons learned here must be applied carefully to other communities. Aboriginal cultures and traditions vary widely across

Australia, and any expansion of this model must be adapted to reflect the specific needs and values of each community.

The broader implications of this program extend beyond child protection. Indigenous young people are also over-represented in the juvenile justice system, and many of the principles underpinning AFDM could be applied to reform in that area as well. Lessons from the program highlight the importance of genuine partnerships between Aboriginal organisations and government agencies, the role of Elders in maintaining cultural integrity, and the need for voluntary participation to ensure that families remain empowered rather than coerced.

At its heart, the AFDM program is about restoring agency to Aboriginal families and communities. While child protection systems must ensure the safety and wellbeing of children, they must also acknowledge the deep wounds left by past policies of forced removal. By embracing culturally appropriate decision-making processes, programs like AFDM offer a way forward—one that prioritises healing, community strength, and the right of Aboriginal families to care for their own children in a manner that honours their cultural heritage.

11

A place in the world for everyone. The closure of Mayday Hills Training Centre[6]

The decision to close the Mayday Hills Training Centre emerged during a reflective conversation between Julie Hind, Manager for Disability Services in the Hume Region, and myself on a return journey from Melbourne. At the time we were consumed by attempts to improve the quality of life for the 200 intellectually disabled residents of the centre. However, the effort faced insurmountable challenges: entrenched mismanagement by the Health Department, underqualified staff, and a deteriorating physical environment. It became evident that meaningful change could not occur within the existing structure. It necessitated an entirely new approach to service delivery.

Mayday Hills was one of two "Joint Facilities" in Victoria, comprising both an intellectual disability training centre and a mental health institution. As the mental health institution was larger and central to the Health Department's core functions, it consistently took precedence over the training centre. Established in 1867 following a Royal Commission into services for the mentally ill and intellectually disabled, Mayday Hills was among the state's oldest institutions, along with its counterpart in Ararat. Both were intended to replace the original 'asylum" at Yarra Bend in Melbourne.

---

6. Appeared in *Broder Mail*, 1997; A fuller discussion of the closure is in Keating TP, (1999) *Institutions in Turbulent Environments*, Ashgate, UK. Reprinted Routledge 2018.

Mayday Hills, historic photo

Although the grounds of Mayday Hills were picturesque, the conditions within the facility were not. The Victorian-era main office, set amidst sweeping lawns, belied the substandard living conditions of the residents. Accommodation consisted of outdated multi-occupant cottages in disrepair and decommissioned former educational department classrooms. Residents had minimal privacy, few personal possessions, and limited opportunities for meaningful activities. Their carers were predominantly psychiatric nurses or mental health aides, most of whom lacked relevant training to support intellectually disabled individuals effectively.

The closure of Mayday Hills occurred gradually between 1988 and 1993. This was achieved by carefully planning individualised transitions, enabling residents and their carers to move together into community-based settings. The process was unlike other institutional closures in Victoria at the time: It was managed almost entirely at the regional level, with limited support, and if fact frequent resistance, from the central office of the Department of Human Services. The closure had to be achieved without transitional funding, meaning that all necessary resources were drawn from within the region or the institution itself.

The success of this transition lay in a partnership between the Department of Human Services Hume Region, the staff of Mayday

Hills, and the staff union. After some initial scepticism, staff had been convinced that their future prospects lay in alternative service models and that the institution's closure was inevitable because no new residents would be admitted. Working groups were formed, drawing on staff members' extensive knowledge of the residents' needs. Agreements were established that guaranteed ongoing employment for all staff, with positions located within a 45-minute drive of Beechworth. Non-direct care staff were funded to undertake training at Wangaratta TAFE, enabling them to transition into direct care roles. Despite their initial lack of therapeutic expertise, staff's longstanding relationships with residents facilitated these changes. Ultimately, staff became enthusiastic participants in the project, and their initially sceptical union became an active contributor. There was negligible absenteeism during the redevelopment, which was unusual during major disruptive change.

The closure was not approached as an organisational or personnel management exercise; its primary goal was to enhance the quality of life for residents and create a sustainable service network for the North East Victorian community. Unlike other institutional closures, no residents were transferred to other institutions. Instead, tailored living arrangements and day activities were developed specifically for each individual. Every resident had a personalised care plan, reviewed by the Victorian Public Advocate, Ben Bodna, who personally travelled to Beechworth fortnightly to chair case planning reviews that would ensure residents received the support they needed, rather than what the department deemed sufficient.

Another significant distinction was the prioritisation of the most challenging cases. The first area targeted for redevelopment was Murtle House, a notorious locked ward where residents exhibited extreme behaviours, and physical and chemical restraints were standard practice. When I first visited Mayday Hills, the manager was reluctant to allow me in to Murtle House to see the boarded up windows and faeces daubed walls with client running around naked and being hosed down in the courtyard. This high-risk decision sent a clear message that everyone, regardless of the severity of their circumstances, had a future. If this initiative had failed, it could have undermined the entire project, but it succeeded, solidifying confidence in the process.

The redevelopment of Mayday Hills was not merely a closure but a transformation. New services were established in locations aligned with future community needs, and the accommodation and day programs were designed to provide high-quality, sustainable support. One reviewer noted that a striking feature of the redevelopment was that everyone involved, staff, carers, and stakeholders, believed that they were personally responsible for its success. This collective sense of ownership was the key to its achievements.

The Premier visits Mayday Hills, 1993

12

Organisational Turnaround in the Department of Community Welfare Services[7]

Turnarounds are not infrequent events for major organisations. Organisations become stale, they lose their sense of purpose and their operating contexts change. It is not unusual to have to refashion organisations, including government departments, in order to meet new and emerging challenges.

There is a lot of management theory about organisational turnarounds, but it is the case studies that can be most informative. One of the most instructive was developed by *ProPublica* and charts the colossal failure of the rebuilding of American Red Cross (ARC). In the mid-2000s ARC was reeling from a sexual harassment scandal at its highest level and had lost the confidence of donors and volunteers. A new CEO was recruited from AT&T communications company, who sacked all senior managers, brought in her own people who had no experience in healthcare or not-for-profits and proceeded to dismantle the volunteer structure that was the organisation's lifeblood. She assumed that the brand was so strong that it could withstand any competitors. She was wrong. ARC lost market share to emerging blood products companies and lost the community support that was integral to its operations. And it lacked the knowledge and skills required to recover its position. The new CEO brought the organisation to its knees.

---

7. First published in Welfare Reflections

Everyone wants to buy a rundown business, or at least to promote it that way. This justifies drastic actions and otherwise unacceptable sackings. It means that any successes can be amplified because of the assumed low base, and failures can be forgiven because the task was so great.

Community Welfare Services (and its successor organisations) had a number of managed turnarounds. In the late 1970s and early 1980's, the Department was the doyen of the Victorian Public Service. It was small, agile and a good fit with the reform politics of the time. Its core business was corrections, juvenile justice and child and family welfare. The Department had been incrementally reforming these: closing the Children's Homes in the comfortable eastern suburbs and around Geelong and establishing locally based family welfare services across the State and de-institutionalising the care of young offenders and wards of the state. It had borrowed the trappings of Whitlam's Australian Assistance Program (AAP) to create what was known as Family and Community Services (FACS); a strategy to develop local coalitions of interest to advance social justice initiatives, using local grants as an incentive. It was driven by a cohort of mostly young, mostly social workers, many of whom trained together at Melbourne University's School of Social Work.

The characteristic strength of the Department and the means by which it harnessed strong operational performance and goal driven policy reform was the nexus between its program development central staff, who were driving new ideas, and strong regionally based operational managers. Central staff and regionally based operational managers shared an interest and understanding of the policy debates and operational effectiveness and respected each other's contributions to shared goals.

The Department was seen as mission focused and robust, capable of making real world changes. As such, it was promoted by the social reformers of the first Cain Labor government, elected in 1982 as a vehicle for major change in the way the state delivered human services. Corrections was transferred out of the department to avoid contamination of new functions. Moved in from a Health Department that was seen as moribund, were children's services, community aged care and intellectual disability services.

A major reorganisation took place. This added some key external people but also lost some important talent. A new Secretary was appointed from the Commonwealth Public Service, whose background was in the regulation of nursing homes and who seemed to some observers, not to understand the Department's functions. The history and culture of the organisation was not understood, and its components were treated as competing power centres rather than collaborating elements of an integrated organisation. An interminable round of meetings substituted for focused action. Intellectual Disability Services were a challenge. Decades of neglect of its residential institutions had allowed abuse to become endemic and fostered a militant industrial environment. At the same time, the Department was taking on a formal role in forensic child protection after the collapse of a non-government service provider. A series of service-related scandals demoralised the organisation and led to a community and government loss of confidence in it. The Department became ripe for turnaround.

Responsibility for the turnaround was tasked to Dr John Paterson. Paterson, an economist and planner, had made his name reforming the Hunter Water Board, transforming it from a loss-making industrial minefield to a profitable well-functioning agency. His achievements were substantial; his marketing of them more so. He bought the 'run down business', Community Services Victoria (CSV) as the department had been named, which he described as "the Beirut of bureaucracy", an underperforming organisational mess that he would transform. For all this talk however, Paterson identified and built on the strengths of the organisation; its intelligent policy analysis and program planning; its capacity for implementing complex reforms and its rigorous operational management. Paterson declared early on that he was going to back operational managers over "the piss and wind merchants" at the centre; he would support people to do things rather than endlessly talk about it. He established a strong organisational model with clear lines of communication and authority.

Paterson affected a robust and at times brutal management style, though in practice his approach was often more subtle and nuanced. He promoted a "scorched earth" approach, tearing down many of the organisation's structures, while relying upon and supporting talented people through the organisation. He valued symbolism and, particularly in the early days, he would send messages by metaphorically taking out and shooting those who he identified as opponents. He did turn the organisation around, though the need for reform was more apparent than actual. Within a short period of time, Departmental officers were acting with authority and confidence, believing that they would be supported through difficult situations.

The scorched earth approach to organisational turnaround is not without its shortcomings. It can lead to an unwillingness to challenge the leader, who is perceived as all powerful and all knowing. Early in his time as Secretary, John Paterson took away the full executive staff group for a management conference in Ballarat. Over two days, he tasked us with giving papers and presentations on the way forward, after which he would deliver his considered view on the priorities. After building suitable tension and expectation, he identified three priorities: the development of an automated child placement system that would match children to vacant beds anywhere in the state; the design and development of one-stop offices that collocated welfare, disability, children's services and housing staff in family friendly environments; and the development of a client services information system that would integrate and make electronic all client records.

The client records system had been in development for three years, but this endorsement gave it a level of support that was needed to complete the project. One-stop shops were worthwhile, though subsequent machinery of government changes reduced their utility. But the game changing centrepiece was to be the welfare booking system. This was a nonsense. We had spent a number of years working towards a child centred approach that carefully matched a placement to a child's assessed needs. The Paterson priority took what was a genuine but peripheral issue, the Friday evening placement crisis, and placed it at the centre of welfare practice, supplanting genuine priorities and core values. All the old welfare hands present knew and understood this and said nothing. The turnaround culture did not allow for discussion, debate or questioning of the leader. The client services information system was duly built with an automated facility for matching placements as Paterson had proposed. That facility was never used in practice.

A further trap with the scorched earth approach is that it encouraged poor imitators. The Intellectual Disability Program was a case in point. Through the 1980s the program was transformed by an alliance of activists and bureaucrats. Institutions were closed or reduced, and local support services were established. Ground breaking rights based legislation was passed. Victoria led the way in Australia and, in some respects the world, in enhancing the rights of intellectually disabled people. The program was chaotic however, with vulnerabilities associated with consumers with challenging behaviours, under-skilled staff and inadequate supervisory structures. Management neglect over decades had transferred power to an aggressive union that had accumulated member privileges.

A new management team adopted the scorched earth approach modelled by Paterson but without his subtlety or intelligence. Following the successful closure of the Caloola residential institution in Sunbury, the majority of the staff who had led that project were moved aside or dismissed. The training program for intellectual disability staff was discontinued. The privatisation of public sector accommodation services was bungled, and operational manuals were prepared by people with no operational experience. After twelve months these manuals had a one per cent compliance rate. The team assigned to turn around the program claimed that its approach was "contentless management". They were correct and it showed. The energy and creativity of the disability program was suppressed and for a time the program became moribund.

Organisational turnarounds are important and sometimes necessary. Successful turnarounds sometimes require radical transformation. Experience, however, would suggest that even organisations that require major change often have core capabilities that are essential to its future operations. Turnarounds can be about nurturing and refocusing that capability, rather than scorching the earth in order to start again.

CSV Senior Management Group preparing for the anticipated change of government, Marysville 1992

13

The nursing dispute and its precedents[8]

Political scientist Hugh Heclo put together what he calls a learning theory of public policy. He examined the fact that the income security systems of Britain and Sweden, noting that despite their commencement at the same time and with not dissimilar social, economic and political fundamentals, they developed in fundamentally different ways. Governments don't only "power" he says, they also "puzzle". The way that social and political systems develop relates less to the rational consideration of evidence than on what went before. Precedence is the great predictor of the future.

The same might be proposed with respect to the current round of health enterprise bargaining in the Victorian health sector and the nurses' industrial dispute which has closed many hospital beds.

The current dispute has its origins in the savage cuts to the health budget initiated by the first Kennett government in 1992/4. That government was elected on the back of the "guilty party" advertising campaign which threw out the supposed profligate Cain/Kirner government. In the pre GST, pre poker machine era, State governments were largely dependent upon stamp duty and payroll tax. In a recession both diminished markedly, and State budgets collapsed. Victoria's financial position suffered in the 1991/2 "recession that we had to have" and also because of the Pyramid Building Society collapse which saw $1.4b taken out of the State's economy. A hapless government had no response to the crisis and

---

8. Published Crikey 2002.

despite the fact that the economy was already recovering by late 1992 and with some relatively minor pruning would have recovered entirely within a few years, the Kennett government was elected with a claimed mandate to slash the public sector.

In Health, cuts of 13% were applied in the first year, using Case Mix funding to apply these rationally. Hospital managers made the cuts where they could. Medical services were largely protected because they drive activity and in fact doctors did very well out of the deregulation of their wage fixing that occurred at the same time and which allowed pattern bargaining. Hotel services (laundry, cleaning, catering) were cut savagely; reserve capacity was removed and nursing numbers slashed. Hospitals were increasingly claimed to be "dirty"; patients spent more time on trollies because there were no beds available for admissions and nurses wilted under the increased workloads. Many apparent economies were ephemeral as direct care staff were replaced by an army of contract managers and outsourcing consultants, who produced no services.

In order to reduce the workforce, retrenchment packages were offered for public servants, and these were taken up in the main by younger staff who had other prospects. The effect was to aggravate the structural problem of ageing in the health and education sectors, the core of which was a workforce recruited in the 1960s and 70s. At the same time the tertiary education sector was undergoing structural change with the out workings of the Dawkins amalgamations and the deregulation of course profiles. Universities found themselves gifted with large numbers of student places in education and nursing which were largely filled by students with middling entrance scores. Prestige in the higher education sector is in part founded on exclusivity and many Vice Chancellors moved to convert these places to more highly sought courses with high entrance cut off scores and for boutique programs which were in vogue, without regard to the workforce implications. The result was that by the end of the 1990s the public sector was facing a largely self-imposed workforce crisis. The core of the workforce was edging towards retirement or was leaving because workplace stress was intolerable; conditions were unattractive and there were insufficient replacement staff being trained.

By the time the Victorian electorate had concluded that its government was too arrogant and self-satisfied and replaced it with the Bracks government in 1999, radical action was required to repair the health workforce system. Wages were improved and government became very active in workforce planning. Victoria's initiatives at this time have formed the basis of the Commonwealth government's approach and the creation of Health Workforce Australia. The most significant development however was the adoption of nurse/patient ratios. The ANF, which had seen the workforce slashed in the Kennett years and the development of intolerable workloads fought a successful battle for ratios to be included in the nursing workforce enterprise bargaining agreement (EBA). The Blair arbitration of this agreement secured a 1:4 ration requirement across the system. It was the cornerstone of the industrial settlement from the Union's perspective and Victorian nurses accepted lower base wages than their interstate colleagues over two Enterprise Bargaining Agreements in order to preserve it. Nurse/patient ratios have subsequently become entrenched in Victorian health workforce legislation.

EBAs come up for renegotiation once every four years. This is the point at which government gets an opportunity to negotiate change. For government nurse/patient ratios are an inflexibility and a cost. While they acknowledge that they have been instrumental in the recovery of nursing numbers, they see the ratios as in impediment to the flexible deployment of the workforce to respond to variability in demand. Their current position is to argue to retain the ratios but with increased flexibility. There is some merit to the argument

For nurses however, the lessons of the 1990s are too current. They have seen that when faced with short term financial constraints patient care and staff wellbeing can too easily be abandoned. An uncompromising ratio which is universally applied and easily monitored is a defence against an employer that cannot be trusted when the times get tough. Nurses will go to the wire for the ratios as they have demonstrated in their defiance on two occasions of directions by Fair Work Australia to lift bans.

The current industrial conflict is not merely an expression of the ritualistic process of negotiation by the parties. It carries the weight of its precedents. The Victorian government health policy during the 1990s was based upon assumptions of the expendability of the public sector workforce and the subservience of patient care to politically determined budget constraints. Now, almost two decades afterwards those assumptions form part of the precedent conditions of current policy stances and conflicts.

14

Gaming the system[9]

When the Kennett government introduced case mix funding to Victorian hospitals in 1993 there was a 17% improvement in productivity in eighteen months. It looked impressive and the government proclaimed its management superiority over that of its predecessors. Much of it, however, was achieved with smoke and mirrors.

In a celebrated circular entitled "Are you dead yet?" the then Secretary of the Human Services Department Dr John Paterson challenged hospital administrators to abandon their public sector ways and start acting as though they were running private corporations. There would be no more bailing out of the inefficient. They would stand or fall on their ability to trade at a profit.

Some of the improved productivity was from cutting costs. Hospitals outsourced hotel functions like linen supply, catering and cleaning and utilised every available bed for revenue generation. Why would you leave a bed vacant for a possible emergency admission when you could fill it with a patient who generated a payment? This led to reports of dirty wards and patients being kept in emergency departments on trollies because no bed was available. Ultimately it led to the removal of the Health Minister Marie Tehan.

The majority of the productivity increase was caused by additional activity. That year hospitals were able to access additional funds from a Commonwealth funded Medicare Additional Throughput Pool. Victoria got in early and gained a disproportionate share in the first year. The next year the other

---

9. Published, Croakey, 2009.

states caught up and the additional money disappeared. Along with it went much of the increased productivity.

But part of the improvement was not new activity, it was just differently coded. In one year, the number of normal newborns admitted went from 13% to 53% and the number of emergency admissions that were discharged within four hours went through the roof. For some reason, suddenly half the children born from non-complex deliveries were so ill that they had to be admitted as hospital patients, and large numbers of people attending emergency departments were so ill that they had to be admitted, but not so ill that they had to stay in hospital for any length of time. The reason was that this generated a higher case payment.

Paterson railed against doctors and administrators who rorted the system. But, in fact, they were only doing what he had urged them to do. Hospital managers were optimising their revenue within the rules as they were. Every subsequent year's funding guidelines for hospitals has seen a rewriting of the rules to plug the latest hole spotted by enterprising operators.

When the former Commonwealth Health Minister sought to introduce the Medicare Safety Net, he was advised that it would inevitably lead to increased costs, particularly for obstetrics. Clinicians are also businessmen. Why wouldn't they restructure their bills so that items previously without charge were billed when there would be no additional charge to their patients.

A recent Victorian Ombudsman's investigation found that a number of Victorian Hospitals had fabricated returns to the Department of Human Services in order to maximise performance incentive payments. But the context needs to be well understood. Hospital administrators who push the purchasing system to its limits have little to gain personally. They are merely trying to keep their hospitals afloat in circumstances where the money available to do so is diminishing in real terms.

The underlying strategy of the Howard government's Health policy was to screw down the public system while subsidising private medicine. This saw the Commonwealth contribution to public health services decrease by 20% over the life of the last Australian Health Care Agreement. State governments increased their share but struggled to keep up with increasing demands and health inflation running at greater than 8%. The funds available for case payments in hospitals are, in their simplest form, the total pool of funds available divided by the amount of activity undertaken standardised for complexity. Limit the pool or increase the activity and you reduce the funds available for each payment.

In the 2009 Budget, the Rudd government has moved to limit and control the application of the Medicare Safety Net, particularly when applied to obstetrics. There has been an implied criticism of doctors who have optimised their income to which both the outgoing and incoming AMA Presidents took exception. But again, their actions are entirely rational given the pricing signals given by an ill thought out Safety Net policy.

Bad policy promotes distorting behaviours. If you provide inadequate funds to sustain the operations of public hospitals, responsible and well-intended administrators will stretch and bend the rules to keep essential public services viable. If you maintain an inefficient fee-for-service medical system with perverse rewards which encourage resource consumption, health professionals will respond accordingly. They are doing what you told them to do!

We would do well to focus on the system that generates gaming rather than upon the individuals who play.

15

Joined-up government – a good idea untried[10]

The recent decision of the Victorian government to separate health functions from community services and housing has been linked to the health reform process and to performance issues in the Department of Human Services.[11]

The reality however is that the health reform process is at the stage of policy debates at the intergovernmental level and the Victorian health system stacks up as more effective than most if not all other States. For all its workload and workforce management problems, Victoria's child protection service is considered a model internationally. So why the change?

The concept of *"Super Departments"* which combine like or related functions into larger administrative units emerged in thinking about public administration in the mid-1980s.

The theoretical underpinning of this was Herbert Simons' ideas on *bounded rationality: We* can be ideally rational, but not about everything and at the same time. We construct our understanding of the administrative world into manageable units and satisfice within their boundaries. These boundaries are constructs not realities and are meaningful for administrators but not for users of services.

---

10. Published Border Mail 2007.
11. The Super Department of Human Services was created by amalgamating the former departments of Community Services, Health and Housing by the Kennett government in 1992. The constituent departments were separated by the Bracks/Brumby government and amalgamated again by the Andrews Labor government. It was disaggregated again after the perceived failures of the department during the COVID pandemic.

Successful complex organisations *differentiate* functions, but they expend comparable effort in *coordinating* between those functions.

A super department would bring together those activities of government that supported health and wellbeing in a way that encouraged coherent policy making across related sectors and promoted integrated service delivery. Or so the argument went.

The Victorian Department of Human Services was established following the election of the conservative Kennett government in 1992. It combined the functions of health (including acute health, primary care, public health and mental health), aged care, community welfare, disability, children's services and housing. The inaugural Secretary of the Department, Dr John Paterson initially put in place a highly integrated administrative arrangement which despite the savage cutbacks of the first Kennett government successfully implemented case-mix funding in the state's hospitals and showed promise of making critical policy and service delivery linkages.

That promise was soon disappointed, however. A decline in public confidence in hospital administration caused by the cutbacks led to a hasty amalgamation of health providers to form metropolitan health networks. These were capital obsessed, resistant to any integration and so large and powerful that they insisted on answering to no-one but the Premier. An old guard in Housing resisted becoming a part of an integrated department and the adoption across the community services and health spectrum of unit pricing and activity based purchasing of services contributed to service fragmentation and myopic policy.

The Bracks government, which was elected in 1999, adopted much of the policy rhetoric of the British Blair government. Brecks's version of joined-up government was set out in *Growing Victoria Together*, an attempt to provide a whole of government policy framework for the State. It was, however, entirely without integrative structures and government departments continued to act in isolation. Super departments like the Department of Human Services and the Department of Victorian Communities singularly failed to integrate their internal program units. In its second iteration, *Growing Victoria Together* proposed to *change the way government works*. It's one mechanism for doing this was regional forums at which government managers might meet. Not surprisingly this weas seen as largely a waste of time.

The need for integrated health and community services policy and service responses is unchanged. Children in care continue to have poor health status; the mentally ill continue to be concentrated in the State's diminishing public housing stock. Victoria's indigenous population continues to experience poor outcomes on all indices of health and community wellbeing. The structure which was to bring together the resources of the state to address those needs has failed to do so.

The failure of the Super Department, joined-up and whole of government experiments was in part a failure in policy. It was also a failure of leadership. Paterson acceded to Kennett's politically motivated amalgamation of metropolitan hospitals and wasted much of his time as Secretary futilely plotting the destruction of public sector unions. His successors acquiesced in the progressive centralisation and fragmentation of program responsibilities and in the end achieved little in the way of joined-up policy or service delivery.

Victoria's current Premier John Brumby is a pragmatist. He has little patience with complex notions of government and believes that outcomes should be delivered simply and quickly. In the circumstances, it is hard to dispute his decision to abandon a failed experiment. Joined-up government has joined that long catalogue of ideas that failed because they were never really tried.

David Green, Public Advocate for Victoria launching my book on the management of change in complex organisations

16

Health Service Amalgamations - the Albury Wodonga experience[12]

Albury Wodonga, one of Australia's largest and fastest growing regional centres, has a combined population of approximately 100k people (including immediate catchments). it is simultaneously Victoria's largest regional centre after Geelong and NSW's largest regional centre after Newcastle. The State border, which dissects the twin cities, masks its significance as a social and economic centre. The Whitlam government's population target of 300k people was scaled back by subsequent governments, and the focus changed from public to private sector growth. Despite this, population growth has continued, particularly in Wodonga, where growth has been sustained at more than three times that of the rest of Victoria for over twenty-five years.

Cross border health provision has been complex and difficult. While the border is entirely porous as far as health consumers are concerned, standalone delivery structures, resourcing constraints, regulatory differences and doctor politics, combined to create difficulties for the effective provision of services. The border area had been unable to harness the substantial buying power of the combined resources of the health providers to maximise workforce recruitment, enhance services or improve quality.

The history of interstate collaboration on cross border health services in Albury Wodonga is long and torturous. A cross-border

---

12. From the briefing to the Interstate meeting of Health Ministers that approved the amalgamation of health services in Albury Wodonga.

study in 1986 examined patient flows and determined that while there was a substantial flow from Wodonga to the then much larger centre of Albury, this was compensated by contrary flows further down the Murray and by tertiary referrals to Melbourne. A further analysis undertaken by Deloitte Touch Ross in the early 1990s, proposed the development of a cross border purchasing authority. Data supporting this proposal was considered unreliable and the proposal lacked local support, particularly amongst doctors. A further study was initiated by then Ministers Tehan and Phillips in 1993. This recommended the establishment of a joint planning committee as a precursor to the development of a single provider, and the consolidation of obstetrics provision at Wodonga Regional Hospital. By the time the report was delivered however, there had been a change of government in NSW, and a new Victorian Minister. Victoria rejected the core recommendations as looking too much like an Area Health Authority, which was contrary to its policy. The integration of obstetrics service proceeded in July 1998.

In 1990 the NSW government opened a rebuilt Albury Base Hospital (ABH) on a greenfield site. It chose to build a 166-bed hospital rather than the 250-bed facility which would have been required to service the entire population of the border area. Victoria was forced to rebuild Wodonga Regional Hospital (126 beds) on its existing site. Relationships between the States on health finance were strained at this time. The Medicare Agreement (later the Australian Health Care Agreement), then provided for payments between the States for interstate transfers. When NSW refused to pay long-standing debts for interstate transfers, the matter went to arbitration. A lower rate was struck, and the total amount payable was capped.

Between the early 1990s and 2006, NSW Health Services underwent significant organisational changes. Albury Base Hospital, as part of the South-West Region, was subsumed successively into the Hume District, Greater Murray Area Health Service (GMAHS) and Greater Southern Area Health Service (GSAHS). During the period 1996 – 1999, severe cost cutting resulted in a significant reduction in the budget of ABH to redress perceived inequities in budget distribution within the Area. The creation of Area Health Services saw the disbanding of local Boards of Management and later organisational changes saw the removal of all Boards. There was a loss of management control of operational activity because of these changes in the organisation of NSW Health. The Area Health Service was in a constant budget crisis, which led to a continuing failure to pay its accounts in a timely manner and a disruption to local businesses. These things contributed to doctors, other health providers, local government and other public and private organisations in the area holding the Area Health Service in near total contempt.

There were significant impediments to the integration of services across the NSW Victorian border:

- NSW and Victoria had distinctly different political and administrative cultures. NSW has a history and practice of centralised authority and control. Victoria has a history and administrative culture of subsidiarity. Victorian public administration assumed that authority and decision-making will be distributed, and that local and regional operatives would be engaged in the framing of policy and service models at a state level.
- The administrative models of the State's health systems were designed to do different things. The Victorian system combined local decision-making with respect to specific outputs, with strong regional and central accountability for price, volume and increasingly for quality. The NSW system took population health as its beginning point and was designed to deliver equity in resource distribution and allocative efficiency with respect to health gain at an Area Health Service level.
- The States utilised different administrative tools. While each State had a similar suite of policy directions, they were reflected in different administrative procedures and practices and different measures of operational performance. Victoria gave primacy to output based purchasing tools, which standardise reporting against benchmark prices. NSW utilised cost weighted separations to measure output and to influence funding allocations, this was less rigorously applied

and operated within an overall population weighted resource allocation. Reporting standards, instruments and language reflected these differences.
- The industrial relations systems were different between the states. Victoria transferred its industrial relations powers to the Commonwealth during the period of the Kennett government. Wages were determined by means of enterprise agreements and local negotiations operated with respect to visiting medical officers. Provision of many ancillary and diagnostic services was outsourced. Employees of Victorian hospitals were at arm's length from government. They operated within the budget sector and conditions are collectively negotiated, but they were employees of their local hospital. NSW operated with a State based centralised wage fixing system and following recent legislative amendment, all health services staff had protected public sector employment. Outsourcing was unusual
- There are countless differences in legal requirements, relevant regulations and administrative practices between the States.

Successful integration

The ultimately successful process of integration commenced in 2001, initiated by the then NSW Minister for Health, the Hon Craig Knowles.

An initial consultancy proposed the establishment, utilising Commonwealth Corporations Law, of a purchasing authority, which would sit above existing providers. These would continue to operate under their respective State legislations, largely unaltered. Victoria rejected this model as adding an additional layer of administration, while doing little to practically advance integration. An Interdepartmental Committee, including senior officers from the central offices of the two state health authorities, as well as the most senior operational managers examined possible governance models, financial modelling, industrial issues, and services planning. Victoria argued for a single entity established under the legislation of either State, or both, if possible, which would have clearly established responsibilities and resources. NSW favoured a contractual relationship whereby Wodonga Regional Health Service

(WRHS) would manage ABH, for an initial three years. A review was to be conducted midway through this period, with a view to the establishment of a legislated model.

The contract entered into provided for the establishment of a Joint Advisory Board, the development of an integrated management team to manage the two facilities, the establishment of a joint Medical Advisory Committee, the negotiation of a single Health Service Agreement which would detail the performance expectations of both Departments, and the construction of a financial management process which would cash flow operating resources to WRHS for the management of ABH. The Contract was to be overseen in a general sense by an Inter Department Committee (IDC) and be managed operationally by a Contract Management Group.

The Contract proved to be a flawed instrument, which largely failed to deliver on expectations for the following reasons:

Issues of risk were inadequately dealt with. Because of the historically bad budget performance of ABH, and the perception that many of the drivers of financial performance would be beyond the control of the integrated entity, Victoria was unwilling to accept responsibility during the contract period for budget risk. GMAHS was unwilling to seriously allow management responsibility to transfer in these circumstances.

- Inability to deliver on undertaking with respect to finance. GMAHS was unable to provide reliable budget figures for ABH particularly with respect to corporate support functions which were performed by Area administration on behalf of ABH.
- Excessive caution. From December 2004, Victoria, urged the immediate establishment of the integrated management team. GMAHS was unwilling to do this because of a concern about how it might be perceived at ABH.
- Distraction by significant operational issues. In the later stages of the contract, considerable organisational energy went into negotiating a common employment contract with Visiting Medical Officers. In the event a common contract could not be agreed. These two operational matters consumed significant time and energy while not progressing integration.

Considerable progress was made however during the contract period. The Joint Medical Advisory Committee was established, and the service plan reviewed. Planning for the establishment of a single emergency department was progressed, though this was frustrated by recruitment issues. Paediatric services were consolidated at both sites, and planning for the integration of pharmacy and of information technology services was advanced.

Albury Wodonga Health

A mid-term review was conducted by Casemix Consulting and came to be known as the Ducket Review. It concluded that while there was significant local support for integration, and considerable benefits could accrue from its success, the organisational model (the contract) was not adequate to the task, and greater support was required from the central offices of the two State Departments. It argued that Health Albury Wodonga should be established as a Public Health Service under the Victorian Health Services Act and that Albury Base Hospital should be funded as a Third Schedule hospital under the NSW Health Act with Health Albury Wodonga contracted for its management. It proposed that the new entity manage the total resources in an integrated way and be funded according to an output based formula along the lines used for Victorian public hospitals. It argued that the new entity should be created by July 2006 but not take up responsibility for service delivery until July 2007, and that the intervening period should be used to manage a transition including the resolution of funding issues and the establishment of appropriate structures. It proposed that the transition be adequately funded, with resources dedicated also at the central levels of Departments to ensure that policy and regulatory support. The fact of the Ducket Review was important in facilitation of progress, though few of its recommendations were adopted.

NSW proposed a more radical governance model, and one which was close to that proposed by Victoria four years previously. NSW Health would excise responsibility for the provision of health services to the Albury Statistical Local Area (SLA) from the budget of GSAHS. It would transfer these responsibilities and budget to the NSW Crown, which would contract with Victoria for the delivery of services to the Albury catchment. The State of Victoria, through the Department of Human Services, would purchase delivery from Health Albury Wodonga in the same way as it does from Victorian Hospitals. A Board of Management would be established, consistent with Victorian legislation, but with equal numbers nominated by each State and an independent Chair. This model had the strong support of Victoria.

The model had several advantages:

- It drew upon the strengths of both Health systems. Victoria's Health care system has well defined purchasing tools and effective delegation of management responsibility supported by regional and central monitoring and accountability. This contributes to a service management system which is efficient. Victoria lacks however, a strong population health culture and a focus on allocative efficiency. NSW was structured for a focus on population health. Resource allocation on a weighted population model with a locational focus, and a capacity to utilise resources flexibly to maximise health gain, has the potential to promote optimal use of scarce health resources. The model proposed service management on a Victorian model with service planning and integration on a NSW model.
- It established clear lines of accountability. Health Albury Wodonga on this model would have one service agreement, with one set of reporting requirements. The NSW contract would be with the State of Victoria, and it would receive reports on performance against that contract from Victoria. The compliance and administrative burden on the provider is thus significantly reduced.
- The model provided for whole of health integration. While the integration project had focused on the acute hospitals, the governance model proposed a way forward for the population of Albury Wodonga, of an integrated provision of all health services. The inclusion of community based health services and mental health in the scope for integration enhanced the clinical outcomes which might be possible as a result of integration.

There were outstanding matters of critical concern to both States during the transition period, prior to the full realisation of Albury Wodonga Health finally announced in December 2009 some three years after agreement had been reached by the States. Both States needed to be satisfied with the financial provisions for the new entity. It was unreasonable that Albury Wodonga Health be required to commence operations with a budget less than its known commitments, and Victoria would not enter into a contract which provided less than the then current cost of operations at Albury. The budget of ABH had not met operating costs for many years, and there was a further discrepancy between budget and the anticipated cost if ABH were to meet its service agreement outputs. NSW had to provide funds more than what might be provided as a share of population.

Risk assignment had to be agreed between the two States. This would be partly addressed if the financial arrangements were satisfactory for both parties. It was not reasonable that Victoria would bear responsibility for risks where those risks might be impacted adversely by the other party. Risk generated by changes in policy or regulation and significant wage movements must remain the responsibility of the contractor.

Industrial relations posed challenges for the new entity and for the two States. The States have different rates of pay and conditions. Different State branches of the same Union cover some aspects of work and in some cases; different unions undertake similar work in different States. The situation is conducive of cherry picking of conditions, and open to demarcation disputes.

Service integration. There was no compelling reason not to proceed with integration of Community Health within the larger catchment but consultation at a community and service provider level was required. Mental Health cries out for integration across the border. NSW however has a disproportion of acute inpatient beds located in Albury and was nervous that integration with Victorian services might lead to demand pressures which might impact upon bed availability for southern NSW.

Conclusions

Political will and active support is a precondition of major cross border projects. Earlier attempts at integration failed because of ministerial changes and the waning of political will.

Projects of this sort challenge multiple personal, professional, commercial, industrial and status interests. An earlier attempt to amalgamate Local Government Authorities in the border area failed because it did not adequately account for the array of interests which could be rallied against it. Achieving and maintaining agreement between a multitude of interests, each with independent sources of power and legitimacy requires an intimate knowledge of the dynamics of local power distribution and utilisation.

Management of change of this sort is politically and technically complex. Each State has its own requirements with respect to industrial relations, occupational health and safety, health purchasing, and quality reporting to name just a few areas of potential conflict. The change management process requires the simultaneous management of change in micro systems, organisational arrangements and the policy environment. It requires strong and sustained leadership at the local, regional and State levels.

Consistency of engagement is critical. It is significant that three of the four members of the IDC were consistent throughout the development of this project, as was the CEO of Wodonga Regional Health Service. This enabled the development of a shared understanding of what was required and a commitment to a successful outcome. The departure of these persons from their positions in 2006 contributed significantly to the further delay in implementation.

Finally, the project reinforced the importance of a focus on the whole of the community of the border area, and the view that it is possible, despite the impediments, to develop an approach, which transcends State parochialism.

17

Maintaining Values in Market Based Care[13]

Public administration systems are not value free. They have embedded within them, assumptions about individuals; about the collective responsibilities of the community and of government; and assumptions about the relationship between government, service providers and individuals who may be in need of care and support.

Relatively recent models of service purchasing, as seen in consumer directed care in aged care and individual consumer plans through the National Disability Insurance Scheme are based upon principles of individuated, contestable purchasing. They herald a new era of accountability of service providers to consumers and as such they are welcomed by most providers.

They also present challenges for community services providers in the context of the evolution of market based approaches to social administration. Current models of human services administration are based on assumptions which underpin a dominant paradigm, often referred to as the "market based approach" to social administration. Not-for-profit service providers, many of which have a history and mission associated with benevolence and altruism may see this administrative model as requiring that they act in ways which are in tension with their organisational rationale.

This paper contrasts the values and assumptions which underpinned what I have described as the "purchase of service"

---

13. Paper prepared for Inner South Community Health Service which received a wide circulation in policy circles.

paradigm and the "market system paradigm" which is becoming pre-eminent in social care administration. It examines some of the assumptions which sit behind the market based system for social administration; some of the challenges these may pose for service providers and some of the strategies that might be useful in addressing these challenges.

How the social administration model evolved in Victoria

The role of government and of service providers in health and community services in Victoria has evolved over time. In the earliest days of the colony/state, the dominant role in the provision of care was assumed by churches and benevolent organisations. The 1850s gold rush created great wealth for some in the community, some of which was transferred over time into benevolence. Government played a limited and residual role, mainly defined by public safety. Prisons and mental health facilities controlled those who might be considered a threat to good order. Scandals associated with the exploitation and abuse of children led to a stronger regulatory role on the part of the state in the early twentieth century but while over time a public hospital system developed, community care continued to be largely delivered by not for profit and religious organisations with little funding support from government.

In the 1960s and 70s, professionalism in the sector increased dramatically and benevolent organisations were no longer able to fund their activities from their capital reserves. The dominant model of resourcing became what might be described as "grant in aid". Government provided for the ill and the disadvantaged by funding not-for-profit and religious organisations which provided services with limited accountability. The State formed a loose partnership with the non-government sector, based on broadly shared goals and an orientation towards altruistic care. This period saw a significant expansion of community based health and community services as government progressively accepted a broader range of responsibilities and the service providing organisations increased their capacity. Community Health Services were established as an alternative to institutional health care, community care for the elderly, mental health patients and people with an intellectual disability. Children's homes were closed across the State and family services developed.

This dominant model changed from the early 1980s as a consequence of the introduction of New Public Management to the management of human services. From a government point of view, the evolution of a new paradigm for the management of human services in Victoria, took place through a number of stages.

Managerialism – developed with the election of the first Cain government in 1983. It required greater reporting and accountability on the part of service providers. Government became interested not just in the fact that agencies did good, but how much good. Funding was however largely based on inputs, such as numbers of funded positions.

Unit purchasing – government purchase from the non-government sector, units of service, often specified in terms of hours of care. This was significant in that it was based upon service outputs rather than inputs. This was a commodification of services which facilitated a market based approach to the administration of care. Units of service could be purchased through a competitive process that placed a discipline on price. Tendering for the delivery of services developed as a favoured means of procurement, justified partly as a means of managing costs but also for reasons of probity.

Individuated care packaging – the latest iteration of care purchasing is based upon consumer controlled care. Purchasing of units of care is undertaken by the consumer or on their behalf by authorised agencies. This has the effect of disaggregating care into service elements and relies upon an overarching care plan to integrate care provision.

These changes in the administrative arrangements of the State were taking place in the context of other developments in the care providing sector from the early 1970s. Monolithic welfare agencies largely moved away from institutional provision and many established regionalised family services which provided family support, in-home care, foster care and small scale residential care. Intellectual disability services, largely run by the State were gradually deinstitutionalised and a not-for-profit sector based on supported accommodation developed. This joined the Day Training Centre sector, a long standing not-for-profit movement which had developed as an alternative to institutional care, to form a significant sector. A community sector also developed with respect to Mental Health Services, again largely as an alternative to institutional care. A strong advocacy by and for people with an intellectual disability and people who experience mental illness, energised community care for the intellectually disabled and the mentally ill. The community health sector developed as an initiative of the Whitlam government and initially saw itself as providing an alternative to a hospital dominated and medicalised health care. Over time it evolved to provide a platform for the delivery of a broad range of community care and health services, frequently in conjunction with hospitals.

Where we have recently come from: the purchase of services paradigm

The purchase of services paradigm was dominant through the 1980s and 90s. It accepted the managerialist framework but balanced this with a communitarian frame of reference. During this period, while the community sector was neither monolithic nor mono-cultural, a number of underlying principles could be identified as common. It asserted:

> ***Localism:*** Scale and location of services is important. Services should be delivered and managed as close as possible to consumers of services. They should be of a comprehensible scale.

> ***A social model of health:*** The causes of social and health issues are at least in part a function of the social and environmental context in which they arise. In addition to individual interventions and care, providers must address

issues of poverty, poor access to resources, marginalisation and disempowerment which contribute to ill-health and social alienation.

Community control of Services: A belief that consumers should have a say in the way services which are important in their lives are managed. Boards of Management should be drawn largely from the communities being served.

Community development as an operating principle: The way in which services are provided should empower consumers and should facilitate collective action to address individual and shared concerns.

Human scale: Services should be delivered in a way which reflects the way people wish to live. This will usually be home-based rather than hospital or institutional care where this is possible and "home-like" residences for those in out-of-home care.

Advocacy as an integral element of care: Self-management is an important part of health and social well-being. Consumers should be supported to manage their own care and to advocate on behalf of themselves. Where consumers are unable to do so, advocacy on their behalf is required, always with their assent.

Universalism: Where possible, services should be generally available to those in the community who require them, without financial impediments.

Priority based on need: Where services are targeted rather than universal, they should give priority to those in greatest need.

Social justice as a priority: The distribution of resources and access to power are understood to be significant contributors to ill-health and social disadvantage. Redressing social and economic inequities is an integral element of social care; and

Social inclusion as an objective of community care: In its stronger form this is an argument about social capital; that the benefits of social interactions and relationships accrue and are available to "invest" in other activities for the collective good. A less strong form would suggest that there are benefits for the individual and for social groups of facilitation of positive social interactions.

The Market paradigm

From a social administration perspective, the emergent dominant model of service purchasing which will be referred to as the market paradigm, reflects the principles of New Public Management. It has a number of underlying principles:

Government steering not rowing. The reform of government activity entailed a redefining of the role of government itself, away from a direct engagement in the delivery of services and towards a policy setting, directing role. While this was in the first instance based upon an assertion that government should take a contingent approach to delivering and managing the provision of care whereby there was a variety of strategies possible, this over time came to be interpreted as requiring that government disengage from delivery and to the extent possible, adopt a purchasing approach only.

Separation of purchasing and providing. The separation of roles is seen as essential for probity reasons and also as a means of promoting efficiency. It is argued that relatively blind purchasing based upon objective criteria allows the development of a more market-like environment relatively unencumbered by established relationships and the legacies of prior delivery. Procurement of services is undertaken on the basis of current rather than past claims.

Competition as a means of driving efficiency. The primary driver of purchasing is efficiency which is most usually expressed in terms of cost, though considerations of sustainability and effectiveness of interventions are also relevant. Competition between potential providers of services is seen as a means of controlling price and this can mean pitting providers, who might in other circumstances see themselves as collaborators, against one another to obtain contracts.

Commodification of care in the form of unitised purchasing. The purchasing of services has required the specification and standardisation of that which is to be purchased. This is most often expressed as units of service: Weighted Inlier Equivalent Separations (WEIS) or hours of home care for example. This has the effect of dissociating the provision of care from the consumer of care and of redefining the role of government and of provider. Government is not responsible for providing care for the homeless but is the purchaser of a specified number of nights or units of accommodation. Service providers are not engaged in the care and support of consumers but are the providers of the numbers of units of services.

Dissolving of the public/private distinction. Where the objective is to provide the defined quantum of services as efficiently as possible, the legal and corporate status of the provider is not of consequence. Claims of special status for "community based" or not-for-profit organisations are not relevant. That an organisation is required to provide a return on capital to shareholders is not of concern to the purchaser.

Consumers as sovereign. The use of market mechanisms can be seen as a means by which the asymmetric power of provers is redressed, and authority is returned to the consumer in selecting a provider. Service providers can be seen as inflexible and unable to respond to the particularity of consumer need, or as monopolistic and concerned to "capture" consumers by limiting their choices of provider and services to be received. This assumes that the consumer is knowledgeable and not so impeded by age, illness or disability to exercise choice. Where this is not the case, agents are authorised to act on behalf of the consumer. This is to describe an idealised application of the paradigm, which may seldom be in operation. For instance, in the community services sector, there is seldom a natural market because there is seldom a pool of potential providers available to compete to deliver services. Strategies to accommodate this have included the creation of internal markets (e.g. Activity Based Funding in Acute hospitals), contracting with or otherwise utilising private sector markets (e.g. COAG public housing reforms) and outsourcing or privatising functions (e.g. disability employment services).

Also, despite the preference for arm's length engagement, competition strategies have frequently been the means by which government has sought to re-engineer the service providing sector. Frequently price is fixed, and competition is not used to drive efficiency in cost terms alone. The Victorian government "recommissioned" the community mental health rehabilitation and recovery services and the Commonwealth is in the process of "recommissioning" the community mental health sector that it funds. This can be defended on the basis that it could increase the efficiency of the sector, but it can also be seen as restructuring the market, favouring large scale over smaller providers and preferencing service outputs over localism and community connectedness.

Tendering can also be used to remove providers who are not considered adequate or who adopt advocacy stances that are in conflict with the purchaser. Competition strategies may be used to restructure the field such that there are fewer providers, or their scope of service is changed.

Issues for the not-for-profit sector in the market based model

The two paradigms described are in tension, though not always in conflict. The not-for-profit sector has generally welcomed management accountability and efficiency in service delivery. Resources saved by efficient and effective delivery are resources available to support consumers. Also, the market based paradigm is so overwhelmingly dominant that it represents the only game in town. If providers wish to continue to provide care services, they must accommodate themselves to this approach. Tensions arise however as a consequence of the disjunction between the underlying values and priorities of market based approaches and the traditional rationale and mission of the majority of community sector agencies. Amongst the points of tension are the following:

Pricing based on averaged costs reduces the viability of providing services to the most vulnerable: Those with higher needs often require more resources in order to reach equivalent goals to those with lesser needs. Where unit prices are uniform or with few gradations, those with the greatest needs may be excluded. There are particular difficulties for agencies which have disproportionate numbers of or who prioritise high need clients.

Advocacy is not valued as a service element to be purchased: Supporting self-advocacy or speaking on behalf of consumers is seldom considered a service output and at worst can be considered an irritant by funding and regulating bodies. For many communities sector organisations, it is fundamental to their social justice goals.

Removal of service need from the social context within which it occurs: Service needs are not understood as occurring within the context of very particular personal, familial and community contexts. An hour of service is an hour of service, and its price is the same, whatever the context. No particular knowledge and understanding of the consumer's environment is required.

Promotion of competition between providers of services for the resources: while providers may collaborate on individual care plans; they will compete for available resources. There is little consideration that one will impact upon the other. Organisational survival can be at stake in completion between providers for program funding.

Detailed specification of service outputs and narrow pricing can leave little discretion and little scope for creative problem solving in the client's interest: where service outputs are tightly defined it can be very difficult to adopt a patient centred approach. Client needs are homogenised with little scope to redefine service outputs to meet their needs. There is evidence for instance that the reduction of funding which accompanied Victoria's recommissioning of community mental health services has seriously limited the development of innovative approaches to mental health services for Indigenous consumers.

Disengagement of providers from the communities they serve: Service providers may not be located within the communities they serve. They may have little appreciation of the nuances of history and culture which have defined communities and impact in a continuing way on the health and wellbeing of members as well as their service requirements. Capacity for consumers to participate in decision making concerning services can be limited.

Reduced connectedness between service elements: Unitised purchasing of discrete service elements requires that these be integrated in meaningful holistic plans. At best this is achieved through "packaged" care plans. At worst, the consumer can be left with unco-ordinated services with unfilled gaps.

The consolidation of service contracts into larger contracts and reduction of the number of providers: Competition favours large scale providers which have the resources and expertise to devote to contestable processes. Recommissioning favours providers who meet the regulating agencies priorities. There are inevitably winners and losers and for some this means they have a reduced or no function.

Introduction of Consumer Directed Care (CDC) in packaged services with disaggregated service elements: CDC is supported by most providers in the community services sector as promoting consumer authority and control over care resources and processes, but it has the potential of realising <u>many of the perceived negative elements of the market driven system. It may result in narrowly</u> defined service provision without community development components. It may be managed at a distance by organisations over which the consumer may have little influence except through the mechanisms of the contract. It may fragment care into poorly integrated elements. It may remove the social and cultural context from service provision.

Separation of authority from delivery: A developing tendency has been for contracted service providers to sub-contract the delivery of service elements such that case management components are retained by the contractor and service delivery is undertaken at a relatively low rate by a local provider. This undercuts principles of local accountability.

Poor industrial outcomes for service delivering staff: The disaggregation of contracts can result in para-professional staff providing care to disparate numbers of consumers with uncertainty over client numbers. This lends itself to the development of a contracted workforce with uncertain income and reduced capacity for collective action.

Infrastructure of organisations not included in pricing: The purchase of units of service does not take account of the physical and organisational infrastructure required to provide care. Where revenue is tied to individual client contracts and where these will vary over time in number and scope, the capacity of providing organisations to plan for infrastructure is diminished.

Strategies for managing in a market environment

Operating within a market related paradigm represents a significant challenge for mission based community services organisations. It requires them to develop a different range of skills to those that they have traditionally utilised. This should not be viewed only in a negative way; not all established approaches are good and the increased level of accountability to consumers that is required in Community Directed Care has the potential to improve service responsiveness. The market paradigm does however represent a challenge to the values base of community services organisations. Clarification of their values and their mission would seem essential in this context. They need to consider the ways in which those underlying values are challenged by the developing environment and the degree to which they are able to compromise without losing their identity and their rationale.

If mission based community services organisations are to maintain their ethical stance they will need, in a robust way, to develop:

> ***Strategies that support a focus upon the needs of the most vulnerable.*** Potentially those who stand to lose most in a market based model of social administration are those who are the least powerful; those whose health and social needs are greatest. Price averaging will always act as a disincentive to providing care for them because the cost of providing to them is very much greater and outcomes are generally poorer. Organisations caring for them must be prepared to see small gains as positive even where these falls well below benchmarks set in contracts.
>
> Strategies that can be considered include negotiation within contracts for segmented pricing rates that better reflect gradations of need; accepting that loses will be made in providing for these clients which will have to be made up elsewhere in the contract and utilising non-contract revenue (such as donations) to subsidise these services. One of the difficulties faced with these strategies is that with CDC or individually packaged services, cross subsidy between clients will be very limited as allocations are to an individual and are acquitted accordingly.

Strategies that promote collaboration with peers in a competitive environment: Collaborative practice within a competitive environment requires a depthing of relationships which goes beyond agreements to work together or even to not compete. It requires an examination with partner organisations of the basis upon which joint activity will take place and the points at which collaboration will not apply. It has been the unfortunate experience of many organisations that consortium agreements are very thin. They are often developed for the purposes of seeking funding rather than guiding action and can result in ill-feeling associated with perceptions of take-overs, exploitation of partners or passivity on the part of some consortium members.

Strategies can include careful negotiation of complementary roles; shared delivery of services on a geographic or functional basis; shared clinical governance or quality management arrangements and agreements about the parameters within which competition and non-competing will operate. It needs to be understood however that in the current competitive environment where government is actively using market approaches to restructure delivery systems through decommissioning and tendering, there will be losers. There will also be providers which are successful in tenders, which are not a part of existing collaborative networks.

There is a role for national and state Councils of Social Services to support frameworks for collaboration between sector organisations and to negotiate with government for purchasing strategies which cause the least possible damage to relationships between service providers.

Strategies that maintain local connectedness: Localism is seriously at risk where recommissioning has an intention of creating larger more capable organisations and where connectedness to communities of interest is not valued. The current tendency for local delivery of services which are managed and controlled at a distance represents a hollowing out of the notion of localism. Service accountability in a community development framework requires local accountability.

Strategies may include segmenting service delivery to reflect client groupings and communities and the maintenance of community engagement structures which enable consumers to have a voice. It needs to be understood however that community engagement without access to actual power is tokenism that will ultimately be rejected by consumers.

Strategies that promote service integration for individual consumers: Unitised purchasing may result in a fragmentation of the services that an individual client requires. In the NDIS and community aged care sectors, care plans are intended to obviate this risk. We know however those community services clients frequently have complex needs and co-morbid conditions. Providing joined up service responses for clients with complex needs has always been a challenge. The possibility that services may be further fragmented by multiple contracts for elements of care, increases this challenge.

Strategies may include the formalisation of shared care arrangements and the nomination of key worker or case manager positions even where this is not a formalised or funded role. The use of inter-agency information management and communications infrastructure may need to be considered.

Strategies that promote service system integration: As services to individuals may become fragmented in a market based environment, so may the service delivery system itself. Services that provide social care for individuals are integrally related to those which provide housing and health services. Contradictory eligibility criteria, service access systems, policies and guidelines can cause havoc in the lives of consumers and cause extreme difficulties for organisations providing services.

Strategies which have been attempted to bring about service system integration have included "joined-up government" approaches in central government agencies and "place management" approaches engaging delivery organisations. Both are out of favour in the current environment partly because they have not been particularly successful, they require an additional administrative overhead, and they run counter to the prevailing orthodoxy which favours state-wide markets for functionally distinct programs.

In the absence of leadership from government, community service organisations may need to establish their own intersectoral working parties to identify systems dysfunction and develop interorganisational approaches to addressing this.

Strategies that promote a social model of health: Social action in the form of client advocacy and action to challenge environmental, social and economic factors that contribute to ill-health, have usually been outside service delivery contracts. They go however to the heart of the understanding that most community services organisations have of their role and how it should be performed. Governments are no longer willing to fund what they see as political activity.

Strategies must firstly acknowledge that this activity on behalf of politically marginalised people is unlikely to be supported through contract revenue. Organisations must be prepared to support this activity and this orientation to their work, by other revenue streams.

Active participation in peak organisations which undertake political activity on behalf of clients and on behalf of the sector may be important in maintaining this focus.

Strategies that optimise scale: The extension of markets for individuated services is enhancing the competitive position of larger scale organisations. Smaller organisations are failing or are being forced to amalgamate. A more explicit discussion about optimal scale and breadth of operation is required. Is there a size of organisation which optimises competitiveness without compromising mission? Can organisations seek to broaden their revenue base by extending their service scope while maintain their focus upon their traditional client groups?

Strategies that reduce costs: One intention of competition is to drive down costs, but many of the strategies to do so which are acceptable in the commercial sector, are seen as unacceptable in the mission-led community sector. These include the exploitation of staff through casualisation and the implied reduction in quality by the use of untrained or unqualified staff. Not all cost savings however need be exploitative or reductive of quality. The use of shared services between organisations, the creative use of technology that enhances the capacity of home based care and the multi-skilling of staff to provide like services across client groups, may reduce corporate costs and enhance both competitiveness and quality of care.

18

The Victorian Nurse Practitioner Program[14]

A substantial body of evidence supported the implementation of Nurse Practitioners in Victoria. While this evidence was not exhaustive and did not conclusively establish that the introduction of Nurse Practitioners would lead to definitive improvements in healthcare quality, it was sufficient to justify their safe integration into the system. The Australian Medical Association (Victoria) (AMA Vic) opposed the initiative on the grounds that its effectiveness had not been conclusively demonstrated and, therefore, should not proceed. However, despite the absence of absolute proof of improved healthcare outcomes, the available evidence suggested that Nurse Practitioners could be implemented safely, offered greater workforce flexibility, and held the potential to enhance service quality.

The impetus for the Victorian Nurse Practitioner Project was largely industrial and vocational, driven by the Australian Nurses Federation (Victorian Branch) (ANF Vic) as a means of improving conditions for its members and expanding the professional scope of nursing. In September 1997, the Victorian Department of Human Services convened a two-day workshop to explore the feasibility of the Nurse Practitioner role. This workshop attracted significant participation, leading to the proposal of a Taskforce to examine key issues, including role designation, educational and legislative

---

14. During 1999, I was Appointed by Minister Rob Knowles to chair the Ministerial Taskforce on Nurse Practitioner and Midwife roles in Victoria, which established the policy to support Nurse Practitioner introduction in the State. This paper was derived from case study material developed with Claudia Trasancos.

requirements, professional indemnity, financial implications, and consumer considerations. The objective was to develop a structured framework for implementing the role within Victoria.

The Minister for Health at the time viewed the proposal as a means of increasing workforce flexibility while addressing industrial relations considerations. Although he was a member of a conservative government, his administration had demonstrated a willingness to enact significant reforms, particularly in health financing, and had been critical of the perceived self-interest of medical organisations. With a substantial parliamentary majority, the government was relatively insulated from public opposition.

The Minister carefully considered the composition of the Taskforce, seeking a balanced representation of stakeholders. Notably, he insisted on appointing a Chair who was neither a nurse nor a doctor. The Taskforce included representatives from AMA Vic, the Royal Australian College of General Practitioners (Victoria) (RACGP Vic), ANF Vic, the Royal College of Nursing Australia, the Nurses Board of Victoria, the Deans of Nursing, and three nursing representatives nominated by the ANF Vic's Nurse Practitioner Forum. The Minister provided explicit instructions that the Taskforce was not to deliberate on whether Nurse Practitioners should be implemented but rather on how they should be introduced. Unlike the New South Wales (NSW) model, which limited Nurse Practitioners to rural areas, or the Canadian model, which confined them to primary care, the Minister sought a systemic transformation unrestricted by geography or field of practice. The Taskforce was required to report within fourteen months, significantly reducing the original timeframe. Consistent with the NSW approach and in line with a commitment to ANF Vic, funding was allocated for demonstration projects to inform the implementation process.

To meet its deadline, the Taskforce convened fortnightly over the fourteen-month period, establishing sub-committees to address its key Terms of Reference, including role definition, educational preparation and credentialling, best practice, professional indemnity and legal liability, legislative amendments, and financial considerations. The Taskforce engaged in collaborative discussions, with active participation from medical organisation representatives.

While AMA Vic initially maintained its opposition—asserting that tasks performed by doctors should not be undertaken by non-medical professionals—its representative nonetheless contributed constructively to the Taskforce's work.

The Victorian Taskforce oversaw the funding and selection of a variety of Nurse Practitioner models to assess their feasibility, safety, effectiveness, quality, and cost, aligning with the evaluation framework established in NSW. These models provided valuable insights into local practice contexts and generated data of national significance. In the first phase, eleven Nurse Practitioner models were funded, followed by eighteen additional models in the second phase. Findings from Victoria were consistent with those from NSW and international studies. The methodology employed mirrored that of the NSW project, incorporating data triangulation from multiple sources. Each project underwent both internal and external evaluations, focusing on access, best practice, appropriateness, cost-effectiveness, and patient outcomes. A Minimum Data Set was developed to standardise data collection across projects. Most projects utilised protocols for diagnostic tests, medication administration, and referrals to other health professionals. In some cases, the Nurse Practitioner role was significantly expanded, with the scope of practice influenced by contextual factors. Structured education programs, incorporating both theoretical and practical training, were implemented, often with substantial support from medical consultants.

Nurse Practitioners in these demonstration projects were widely accepted by their professional colleagues and patients. Nursing professionals perceived the role as an enhancement to their profession and as supporting interdisciplinary collaboration. Client perception surveys indicated overwhelmingly positive feedback regarding the quality of care, attention, and expertise provided by Nurse Practitioners. Case study findings confirmed that the role was well-received across a range of healthcare settings, and Nurse Practitioners were highly valued by both colleagues and patients.

However, the evaluation process posed challenges for the Taskforce, particularly regarding the evidence base for implementation. The fourteen-month timeframe encompassed both project establishment and evaluation. The administrative requirements of defining project specifications, assessing proposals, and launching demonstration projects were substantial, with many projects only commencing six months into the Taskforce's operation. Consequently, the evaluation of first-phase projects, based on limited data collection periods, was primarily descriptive and contributed little to the Taskforce's deliberations.

The Taskforce submitted its final report in December 1999, presenting thirty recommendations for the implementation of Nurse Practitioners. These recommendations represented the most progressive Nurse Practitioner implementation model in Australia and were aligned with international best practices. Consistent with the Minister's vision, the report recommended statewide implementation without restriction by practice area and proposed systemic funding through existing healthcare funding models rather than through designated positions. This approach was intended to ensure that Nurse Practitioner roles were introduced based on demonstrated need and effectiveness rather than political expediency.

As the report was finalised, AMA Vic reaffirmed its opposition, formally dissenting from key recommendations. RACGP Vic aligned itself with AMA Vic, particularly in objecting to the removal of the "locally agreed need" criterion for establishing Nurse Practitioner services, a requirement that granted local medical practitioners the power to veto such roles under the NSW model.

The Evidentiary Basis of Policymaking

The extent to which health policymakers and managers should adhere to the same evidentiary standards as clinicians is a subject of debate. Walsh and Randle (2001) highlight the challenges policymakers face, including the overuse, underuse, and misuse of initiatives, as seen in the rapid adoption and abandonment of trends and the slow uptake of genuine innovations. They argue that differences in culture, context, and methodological approaches distinguish the policymaking domain from clinical practice, which is more precisely defined and methodologically rigorous. Moreover, management decisions are shaped by organisational and systemic constraints, including resource availability, market pressures, institutional policies, and stakeholder interests.

The implementation of Nurse Practitioners in Victoria occurred within this complex policymaking environment, influenced not only by clinical evidence but also by structural, economic, and political considerations. While substantial evidence supported the safe integration of Nurse Practitioners, AMA Vic contested the validity of this evidence, asserting that it was largely qualitative rather than derived from randomised controlled trials—the gold standard in medical research. Beyond methodological concerns, there was a broader issue of professional territoriality, with AMA Vic resisting any delegation of medical tasks to non-medical professionals.

Tuohy argues that opportunities for policy change in healthcare arise from broader political contexts rather than from within the health system itself. In the case of Nurse Practitioners in Victoria, a convergence of interests among government officials, nursing organisations, and community health advocates enabled implementation, despite resistance from the medical profession. However, following the 1999 election, a newly elected minority government, wary of major structural changes, adopted a more cautious approach. Under intense lobbying from AMA Vic, the government imposed stringent regulatory and legislative requirements for Nurse Practitioner endorsement, potentially creating long-term barriers to the profession's expansion.

Ultimately, the Victorian experience underscores the interplay between evidence, policy, and political negotiation in healthcare reform. While the nursing profession pursued greater autonomy and professional recognition, the medical profession sought to maintain its influence. The debate over Nurse Practitioners became not merely an issue of evidence but a contest over professional authority and systemic control in healthcare policy.

Section 3: *Builder not sacker, your shield the mortar board*

Trowel-wielder, woundie, drive them off
Like Odysseus in Hades lashing out
With his sword that dug the trench and cut the throat
Of the sacrificial lamb.
But not like him—
Builder, not sacker, your shield the mortar board—
Drive them back to the wine-dark taste of home,
The smell of damsons simmering in a pot.

Seamus Heagney: from Damson

19

Communalism and Disaster Recovery[15]

An exploration of disaster recovery theory and practice has led to a range of significant, albeit sometimes uncomfortable, conclusions. Specifically, a reflexive approach to communalism in disaster recovery processes reveals critical insights that warrant deeper analysis.

One key issue concerns the widespread adoption and conceptual ambiguity of communalism in disaster recovery. The former appears imminent, if not already established in several jurisdictions, while the latter is endemic both within this specific field and more broadly. Marsh and Buckle (2001), compellingly argue that the concept of 'community'—the predominant expression of communalism in practice—is frequently misused and misunderstood within the contexts of risk management, emergency response, and recovery. They acknowledge that 'probably there is no such thing as "the community"' while simultaneously emphasising the necessity of defining the term. This contradiction suggests that the discourse surrounding community requires more than definitional clarity; rather, its conceptual confusion demands rigorous social analysis.

From a sociological perspective, conceptual confusion is not merely an obstacle to be resolved but a phenomenon to be examined in its own right. Instead of striving to eliminate ambiguity, we should interrogate why such confusion persists, how it is maintained, and, crucially, what broader social functions it serves. It is worth considering why a term as nebulous as 'community'—lacking

---

15. Derived from a paper given jointly with Prof Kit Carson to the International Research Committee on the Sociology of Disasters, Brisbane, 2002.

conclusive empirical validation of its effectiveness—continues to be central in disaster recovery discourse. The meanings, applications, and even misunderstandings of 'community', along with related constructs such as social capital and civil society, are deeply embedded in social contexts. Consequently, their significance cannot be determined solely through theoretical debates but must be examined through empirical social analysis.

This line of inquiry aligns with Quarantelli's assertion that disasters in contemporary Western societies are 'embedded in the social dynamics of developed societies'. Thus, we must critically examine why community and its affiliated concepts are deployed so enthusiastically yet ambiguously in disaster recovery. What does this reflect about broader socio-political trends, and what might it obscure? Higgins (2001) suggests that the concept of community plays a role in shifting the burden of risk in Australian drought policy, moving it from the realm of state responsibility to that of individual farmers. During the 1990s, drought policy evolved from being primarily a social governance issue—where the government was responsible for natural disaster response—to a hybrid framework in which farmers were expected to manage 'manageable risk', with the government intervening only in cases of 'exceptional circumstances'. In this shift, community functioned both as a governance technology and as a mechanism for redistributing responsibility.

While Higgins acknowledges the role of community in this transformation, further examination is warranted. Our own research suggests that in two separate disasters—a bushfire and a drought-flood emergency—community-oriented recovery programs played a significant role in transferring risk from the state to individuals. Similarly, preliminary discussions with officials from Victoria's Country Fire Authority indicate that the 'Community Fireguard' program, while commendable for its approach to fire preparedness, may also facilitate the delegation of risk management responsibilities to individuals. Whether such programs merely reflect or actively obscure shifts in responsibility remains an open question, as does the extent to which these trends align with Dynes' (2000) call for integrating disaster awareness into the daily routines of individuals, organisations, and communities.

More broadly, the widespread emphasis on community in disaster recovery policy signals a shift not merely in technical approaches but in the fundamental governance of disaster management. This shift reflects a movement away from state-centred responsibility and towards the responsibilisation of non-state actors, including individuals and local collectives. Whether this trend represents the triumph of neoliberalism or an emergent structural pluralism is, in one sense, immaterial; in either case, it signifies a realignment of disaster recovery policy with the evolving rationalities of governance in late modern society.

Understanding the embedded nature of community and social capital within these governance structures is crucial to assessing their popularity, confusion, and ambiguity. Addressing these issues is a pressing research imperative, arguably more so than engaging in another round of definitional debates, which may ultimately prove futile.

A further fundamental issue concerns the efficacy of communalism in disaster recovery. Does communalism, in any operationalised form, actually facilitate effective recovery? Disaster recovery research must move beyond ideological enthusiasm and towards empirical scrutiny, disentangling correlations from causal relationships. If communalism is positively associated with successful recovery, can we distinguish between pre-existing communal capacity and that which is generated through intervention? If such a causal link exists, what mechanisms drive it? Conversely, might other contextual factors be responsible for observed associations between communalism and recovery outcomes?

These questions are significant. If no convincing relationship can be demonstrated, critics may argue that concepts such as social capital are inherently flawed as foundations for public policy. Even if positive associations are established, interpretation remains complex. At one extreme, community-based recovery programs may enhance communalism, which in turn drives recovery. At the other, an independent variable may simultaneously influence both communalism and recovery without any direct causal link between them. Additionally, disasters themselves may alter levels of social capital and communal engagement in unpredictable ways. The complex interplay between these factors underscores the necessity of rigorous empirical investigation.

Assuming a positive relationship exists, identifying its components is vital for informing policy. If pre-existing communal structures are key to recovery, then high-risk areas should be targeted for community capacity-building initiatives that extend beyond traditional disaster preparedness programs. Such an approach would necessitate a 'whole-of-government' response, integrating multiple agencies across sectors such as education, health, and human services. This, in turn, has implications for bureaucratic structures, challenging traditional silos and necessitating cross-sectoral collaboration.

Even if communalism proves effective in disaster recovery, we must interrogate its explanatory power. For instance, attributing slow recovery in a struggling rural logging town to 'low social capital' ignores the broader economic forces at play, such as globalisation and industry decline. Communalism is socially embedded and failing to recognise its structural determinants risks misdiagnosing the true barriers to recovery. This is particularly pertinent given the tendency of social capital discourse to overlook issues of power, inequality, and exclusion.

The broader implications of communalism in disaster recovery extend to questions of democracy and governance. Do participatory and community-driven recovery initiatives genuinely empower affected populations, or do they merely serve as mechanisms for legitimising preordained decisions? To what extent do existing political structures facilitate meaningful community engagement, and are new mediating institutions required? Such questions demand careful scrutiny, particularly in light of critiques that current participatory frameworks may amount to little more than symbolic consultation.

Similarly, accountability must be reconsidered. As Twigg and others have noted, disaster management professionals often prioritise 'upwards accountability'—to donors and governments—over 'downwards accountability' to affected communities. This imbalance must be addressed if communal recovery frameworks are to fulfil their democratic potential. One promising avenue is participatory evaluation, in which affected communities actively contribute to assessing recovery programs. This approach not only enhances accountability but also facilitates the co-production of knowledge, moving disaster research away from an expert-dominated paradigm and towards a more inclusive epistemology.

Ultimately, disaster recovery expertise must be reconfigured to accommodate democratic decision-making and collaborative knowledge production. This entails profound shifts in both bureaucratic practice and research methodologies. Traditional positivist approaches, while valuable, must be complemented by constructivist methods that acknowledge the contingent and context-dependent nature of recovery. Disaster managers and researchers alike must cultivate reflexivity, recognising their role within broader governance structures and embracing the complexities of late modernity.

While communalism in disaster recovery presents both opportunities and challenges, a reflexive and empirically grounded approach is essential for realising its potential. By critically examining the intersections of community, governance, and disaster management, we can move beyond ideological commitments and towards more effective, equitable, and democratically accountable recovery frameworks.

20

Mental illness and compassion[16]

There is a story, perhaps apocryphal, told about Francis of Assisi. As a wealthy young man, he would often ride from his home and pass a group of lepers. Being a young man of conscience and compassion, he was embarrassed at his practice of skirting around them. Seeing a leper near naked, he gave him his coat. He continued on but was still uneasy. When he rode past next day, he dismounted, and rather than just give his coat, he embraced the man.

We long ago ceased to see leprosy as unclean and banish its sufferers. We've learned to treat the ill with care and compassion and not to fear them - or have we?

One and five people experience some form of mental illness during their life, most commonly depression and anxiety. About 3% of Victorians at any one time will require treatment and support due to serious illness. Mental illness is experienced by people in our families, and our workplace. It's not something which affects only an isolated group of people who can somehow be kept apart from the rest of us.

For some years Australian governments have been committed to the principles of a national mental health strategy. These principles are about bringing mental health services into the wider health system, and about directing funds to community treatment.

Public mental health services in Hume region are now managed by general hospitals and two thirds of funds are spent on

---

16. Appeared *Border Mail*, 20 May 1996.

community based services. The movement of funds is just catching up with the movement of treatment patterns. In the past, funds have been locked up in old style institutions like Mayday Hills. An increasing proportion of funds is now being spent in the community where treatment occurs. At least 85% of people with serious mental illness are treated and supported in the community. This has been the case for many years. In Victoria, people admitted to acute psychiatric units. stay on average 15 days. Delivery of services in the community is usually more effective and it's not as disruptive for those who are ill, their families and carers, as treatment that is outside their community.

By emphasising treatment in a community based mental health service, people with a serious mental illness, gain greater involvement in community life and increased independence and they are assisted to maintain their daily living skills. They also have a greater contact with family and friends, and have a better chance of retaining their job, home and social networks, all of which aids recovery.

Community mental health services like the Wodonga District Psychiatric Service are the cornerstone of community base treatment. They provide a wide range of clinical assessment, treatment, and support functions for people with the mental illness and their families. Since early this year the service's crisis service has been contactable seven days a week 24 hours a day. The service will arrange admission to hospital if necessary. There will always be a small minority of people who require extended care in a supportive environment. Community care units provide the opportunity for people to live in a homelike environment with support from health professionals 24 hours a day. This is the type of service planed for units in Wilson St Wodonga.

Mental illness covers a very wide spectrum, including depression, anxiety, disorders, schizophrenia, and bipolar illness. Schizophrenia is one of the most devastating misunderstood mental illnesses. There are some common misconceptions.

It is not rare, one in 100 Australians might develop it at some time. It is about six times more common than insulin independent diabetes and 60 times more common than muscular dystrophy.

Schizophrenia has nothing to do with so-called "split personality" as often assumed. It is an illness which affects the brain, causing hallucinations, delusions, disorder, and other symptoms.

Another misconception is the people with schizophrenia are likely to be violent. Research shows that people treated for schizophrenia are no more prone to violence than the general population, they just get blamed more by the media.

That people with schizophrenia cannot be helped is a further misconception. There is no cure yet, but it is a treatable illness. Some people recover with proper medication, rehabilitation and support. Many others are able to lead satisfactory lives in the community. This is especially so when they receive understanding from those around them and are treated as people with schizophrenia rather than schizophrenics.

Many people are frightened of people with mental illness. A sad truth however is that it is often those who are mentally ill who live in terrible fear and confusion because of their illness.

Is it too great an ideal that we might show tolerance for those who are different, compassion for those who are ill and support for our friends, our families, and our colleagues when they need it?

We can ride on by and avoid those who need our help, or we can give them the material support they need.

Better, still we can, like Francis, embrace them as members of our community.

21

Hallelujah[17]

I take Leonard Cohen's song *Hallelujah* as our beginning of our discussions and plans for the future.

It is a work of profound beauty, rich in Judaic and Christian imagery, that speaks deeply to who we are. I believe it also has something important to teach us about our work.

Cohen describes David as a "baffled" king. There is much to be said for bafflement—for uncertainty, for openness to possibility. In the caring professions, however sincere our motivations, there can be a tendency toward triumphalism. We stand apart from those we serve, doing things *to* them or *for* them, secure in our role. Our hallelujah, our song of praise, can become steeped in satisfaction, in self-assuredness.

But the reality is that most of those we serve live their lives in a minor key. Perhaps we, too, should spend more time being baffled. I have long been uneasy with the familiar Jesuit formulation of a mission "to the poor," as it risks objectifying those we seek to serve—assuming *they* are poor while *we* are not.

Cohen's song interweaves the sacred and the profane, revealing them as one.

> *Your faith was strong but you needed proof*
> *You saw her bathing on the roof*
> *Her beauty and the moonlight overthrew you*

---

17. Address to open Jesuit Social Services Strategic Planning conference, February 2007.

> *She tied you to a kitchen chair*
> *She broke your throne, and she cut your hair*
> *And from your lips she drew the Hallelujah*

Whether it is King David undone by his desire for Bathsheba or Samson by Delilah, their glory emerges *through* the realisation of the brokenness of their nature.

Our nature does not call us to personal aggrandisement.

> *I've seen your flag on the marble arch*
> *Love is not a victory march*
> *It's a cold and it's a lonely Hallelujah*

Cohen's vision is strikingly Buddhist. Peter Steele's fine poetry and sermons, are Augustinian in their provenance. Their beginning stance is, " we stand in the gutter with our eyes to the stars". Cohen's vision is different: we are not *in* the gutter—we *are* the gutter and we are the stars. Our hallelujah is a song of celebration of that.

I believe he is telling us that our calling to greatness, our hallelujah, will not arrive like Samuel's voice in the night or Paul's blinding light on the road to Damascus.

> *It's not a cry that you hear at night*
> *It's not someone who's seen the light*
> *It's a cold and broken Hallelujah*

It is revealed in our brokenness. We respond to our god however we understand that, not through strength, but through the recognition and celebration of our essential brokenness , understanding that this is not something we occasionally feel, but that it is who we are. And that is true whatever our tradition:

> *There's a blazing light in every word*
> *It doesn't matter which you heard*
> *The holy or the broken Hallelujah*

And if we start to understand brokenness as both deeply human and also sacred, we will understand others differently. In seeing the vulnerability and brokenness of others, we see their glory, their inherent song of praise. If we understand this, our approach to service will be fundamentally changed.

So let us proceed with our planning in the spirit of bafflement and embrace the brokenness that is essential to who we are and let us understand that every broken person is a prayer.

22

Multi-disciplinary Training for Mental Health[18]

Research highlights several challenges in implementing effective multidisciplinary training in mental health. One key issue is the difficulty in establishing a common understanding between psychiatrists and primary care physicians. There is a need to rethink the traditional roles and responsibilities of different professional groups.

Training is essential for professionals who are part of multidisciplinary teams or those increasingly required to support people experiencing mental illness in general health and community settings. This need has arisen due to the integration of psychiatric and mental health services into broader healthcare systems.

The shift towards a holistic approach to healthcare, combined with changes in care models and the prioritisation of primary care, has driven the development of interprofessional education in mental health. As a result, healthcare professionals must increase their knowledge of mental health treatments to address a wide range of patient needs, including dental care and psychiatric rehabilitation. Special attention has to be given to training non-psychiatric professionals such as general practitioners, emergency triage nurses, dentists, pharmacists, correctional workers, social workers, and emergency department staff. The literature notes that pharmacists may hold negative stereotypes about mental illness, which training programs should work to address.

---

18. Advice provided to the Department of Health and Aged Care, 2008.

Rural mental health services face unique challenges and require specific training strategies to improve communication and collaboration between service providers. Additionally, training programs must consider the particular needs of staff working in correctional services. The reluctance of some primary care physicians to engage with mental health care suggests that more targeted training is required to build confidence and competence in treating psychiatric illnesses.

Many examples of effective multidisciplinary training programs exist, particularly in undergraduate education. The success of these programs relies on strong relationships between educational institutions and service providers. Common training goals include improving team communication, resolving power conflicts, clarifying professional roles, and developing shared therapeutic models.

Post-qualification programs often focus on fostering shared learning experiences among professionals from diverse backgrounds. Training content typically covers evidence-based psychosocial interventions, collaborative approaches to working with mental health service users, cognitive-behavioural strategies, reflective practice, clinical supervision, and medication management. Some programs also explore the use of new technologies to enhance training delivery.

Specialised training initiatives exist for staff in acute care settings, ensuring they are equipped to support patients with acute or chronic mental health conditions. These programs involve a mix of lectures, group discussions, site visits to community-based treatment facilities, and supervised clinical practice. Other training models include multidisciplinary practicums, clinical supervision, and service-based training in areas like marriage and family therapy and public child welfare.

Research evaluating multidisciplinary training in mental health has found several benefits. These include improved team functioning through structured treatment planning sessions, enhanced collaboration between professionals, and better assessment skills and clinical practice. Training programs have also been linked to positive outcomes in emergency department settings, including improved team behaviour, reduced clinical errors, and better management of care for domestic violence victims.

Internationally, the United Kingdom has led the way in interprofessional education in mental health, particularly in primary health care and nursing. The literature suggests that training should move beyond skill development to establish shared therapeutic models among professionals. Training content often emphasises knowledge and skills in psychosocial interventions, while new learning technologies support workplace-based education, particularly for rural practitioners.

Studies have shown that interprofessional education improves team relationships and performance. Practical training approaches, such as multidisciplinary field practicums and cross-professional clinical supervision, are particularly beneficial. By fostering collaboration and shared learning, these programs help improve mental health care delivery and outcomes for patients.

23

Non-medical prescribing[19]

Non-medical prescribing has traditionally been dominated by doctors, both in Australia and internationally. Over time, however, workforce shortages, the expansion of advanced practice among other health professionals, and the shift towards more collaborative healthcare models have placed pressure on this traditional approach. In response, alternative prescribing models have emerged to improve access to medications, particularly in rural areas, aged care, Indigenous health, and chronic disease management.

Other countries including the United Kingdom, New Zealand, Canada, and the United States have introduced non-medical prescribing to address service gaps. The United Kingdom has been at the forefront, allowing trained nurses, pharmacists, and podiatrists to prescribe independently within their areas of expertise. In contrast, Australia has maintained a more limited approach, primarily linked to the role of nurse practitioners, who are often restricted to specific prescribing lists and face funding barriers that limit their ability to practise as freely as their international counterparts.

There are three main approaches to non-medical prescribing. Independent prescribing allows a trained health professional, such as a nurse practitioner or pharmacist, to take full responsibility for assessing, diagnosing, and managing a patient's treatment, including issuing prescriptions. Dependent prescribing involves a

---

19. From a paper prepared for the Commonwealth Department of Health and Ageing, 2014.

doctor delegating prescribing authority, often in a setting such as a general practice clinic where nurses work under medical supervision. A third approach, collaborative prescribing, requires a structured partnership between a prescriber and a doctor, often used in managing chronic conditions where coordinated care is essential.

The application of these models varies across different countries. In the United Kingdom, non-medical prescribing is well established, with nurses and pharmacists able to prescribe a wide range of medicines, including some controlled drugs, following structured training and supervision. In New Zealand and Sweden, the introduction of non-medical prescribing has primarily focused on improving healthcare services for elderly patients and those receiving nursing care in the community. In North America, non-medical prescribing is linked to the roles of nurse practitioners and physician assistants. The extent of prescribing authority in the United States varies by state, with some allowing full independence and others requiring oversight from a doctor. In Canada, clinical assistants and nurse practitioners play similar roles, with prescribing authority typically linked to specific guidelines and regional regulations.

In Australia, non-medical prescribing has primarily been implemented through nurse practitioners and a limited number of allied health professionals, such as optometrists and physiotherapists, who have narrowly defined prescribing rights. Unlike in the United Kingdom, where non-medical prescribing is widespread, Australian nurse practitioners often face barriers to practising independently due to restrictions on access to Medicare and the Pharmaceutical Benefits Scheme. These funding limitations impact the ability of nurse practitioners to provide cost-effective care, particularly in areas with fewer medical professionals.

As Australia's population ages and the demand for primary healthcare services increases, the need for a more flexible prescribing system has become evident. Non-medical prescribers, particularly nurse practitioners, have played a crucial role in chronic disease management, palliative care, and mental health services, where their ability to provide timely medication access is essential. Despite this, structural and policy constraints continue to limit their full integration into the healthcare system.

24

Rural Hospitals and Structural Change in Health Care[20]

Institutional health arrangements are integrally related to the structure and functioning of rural communities. Rural hospitals provide access to critical services influencing personal well-being and they are frequently significant employers within the community. Their presence is often a factor in the availability of ancillary services such as pharmacy and general practitioner services. Small rural hospitals also play a critical role in the history and memory of communities, often being the location of significant family and community events such as births and deaths. As such they attract fierce community loyalty and, in many cases, have been the symbols of community resistance to change.

Changes in medical technology, demography and health financing policy have inevitably led to a change in the demand for, and the viability of small rural hospitals. The process of effecting structural changes in these services, in addition to the actual changes themselves have frequently been difficult for rural communities.

It is tempting to think about the changes being faced by small rural hospitals in terms of responses to single political events such as changes to the purchasing arrangements for their services. It is important to understand however that these hospitals are dealing with large scale and interrelated changes in the general environment. These include changes to the technology of health care, such that complex medical treatments have become

---

20. Extract from an article published in the Journal of Rural Social Work, April 1999.

concentrated in major provincial centres and in metropolitan referral hospitals, and demand for bed based care in small rural providers has diminished.

Increasingly treatment can be provided in individuals homes as an alternative to admission to hospital. There are changes to the political environment, particularly in relation to health financing, and cultural changes, represented by changed demography, employment, accommodation, and transport patterns. These factors taken together, presented a highly connected and dynamic environment commonly referred to as turbulent.

A distinguishing feature of turbulent environments is a difficult for an organisation to influence or to modify because they consist of elements which have a powerful determinative effect on the organisation but are beyond its direct relationship. Further, changes in a turbulent general environment can be such that the organization, in this case a hospital, may have difficulty obtaining information or in comprehending the changes taking place.

Change processes do not occur in isolation. They build upon the histories of organisations and of communities, and they modify those histories. In order to understand the responses of the hospital to the changes it faces, it is important to understand the community in which it is a significant institution.

Managing change in a turbulent environment requires substantive leadership of the change process.

The interorganisational field is critical as one of the contexts within which changes in rural health configuration takes place. Changes within individual healthcare providers in rural communities cannot take place without significant repercussions for other organisations. This is frequently understood in terms of the impact of reductions in acute hospital services upon the availability of medical practitioners and ancillary services such as pharmacy within communities.

There is no doubting the potential losses associated with the reduced viability of services which rely upon acute hospitals to maintain work volumes. The impact on the interorganisational field, however, are more complex than this. Changes in the roll of one provider in a rural community, however small, have implications for other providers. General practitioners may have structured their practices around the operations of a traditional hospital. A practice may be located adjacent to the hospital. They may receive a direct subsidy from the hospital for their on costs. More significantly a change in behaviour by the hospital away from admission to bed basic services towards bed based home care would require major changes in their practice methodologies; changes that they may be slow to make. Changed roles may have implications for regional as well as local providers.

A further complication to relationships within the interorganisational field is that environments are seldom static. Turbulent environment by definition continue to change. Agreements and negotiated roles are perishable as the context continues to change.

Change is inevitable and inexorable in rural health care provision. It is not possible to ignore it or oppose it. It is possible to understand and to manage it however, in such a way as to create improved outcomes for rural communities. To do that, it is important to understand the nature of the impending change, its internal implications and its implications for the interorganisational field.

25

Incentives for Rural Health Employment[21]

There is a shortage of skilled workers across many professions in Australia, and this is a major concern for health workforce planning. While the shortage is affecting the whole country, rural and remote areas are expected to face even greater challenges. These shortages could have a significant impact on the delivery of health services in these regions.

As a contribution to addressing this, a study was undertaken to review the policies used to attract and retain workers in rural and remote areas. The aim was to help the Australian Government plan for future workforce needs in regional and rural Australia. A key focus of this project was to examine how financial incentives could help attract and keep professionals in these areas. This included looking at whether extra payments were needed to encourage people to move to rural areas, how much more rural workers earn compared to their city-based counterparts, and what non-financial benefits, such as extra leave, were offered. The study also assessed the value of these incentives.

The research explored key issues such as the importance of salary differences, other work-related entitlements, and additional benefits beyond financial incentives. To gather information, the project involved a detailed review of Australian and international research on recruitment and retention strategies. This included academic studies and industry reports. The review aimed to

---

21. Advice provided to the Department of Health and Ageing, 2007.

identify key factors that influence workforce attraction and retention, strategies used across different industries, how success is measured, variations across sectors and locations, and which approaches have worked best.

Structured interviews were also conducted with representatives from professional associations, government agencies, employer organisations, recruitment consultants, unions, and major employers. These interviews provided insights into job availability, recruitment challenges, salary differences, additional benefits offered to rural workers, and other non-financial incentives.

The study confirmed that a skills crisis is affecting most of the professions examined, with the situation being particularly challenging in rural and remote areas. The combination of a booming resources sector and a skills shortage has made it difficult for some industries to attract and retain workers. As a result, competition for workers has driven up salaries and benefits.

In the resources industry, traditional definitions of rural and remote do not always apply, as companies often use a site-based approach. A key observation across industries was that recent graduates have higher expectations than previous generations. They are motivated and eager to contribute but also expect strong leadership, flexible work conditions, and opportunities to gain diverse career experiences.

Understanding the market dynamics of different sectors is crucial in designing workforce strategies. Employment factors within communities are closely connected, meaning that challenges faced by one employer can affect others.

Various incentive strategies are being used across different industries. These include direct financial benefits, job design and restructuring, professional development, and personal or family-related incentives. In terms of salaries, companies in the resources sector generally pay about 20% more to workers in field locations compared to city-based employees. In the public sector, extra payments and benefits range from 7-20% of salary, while in the resources sector, they are between 17-28%.

Public sector workers may be eligible for regional allowances, but these payments have not been updated for a long time and do not accurately reflect the higher cost of living in rural areas. In the resources industry, there is a difference between fly-in/fly-out operations and roles requiring workers to live locally. Across all industries, salary is important, but workers also value the overall job experience, including non-financial benefits. The most significant additional benefit in the resources sector is accommodation, while in the education and health sectors, some subsidised government housing is available, though the support is relatively small. Concerns about the quality and availability of housing were raised across industries.

Public sector agencies are facing increasing difficulties in competing with the well-resourced and flexible private sector. A safe workplace was identified as a key factor in attracting and keeping employees. The skills shortage has led to changes in employment models, such as more fly-in/fly-out roles in the resources sector and an increase in automation, where operations are managed remotely.

Many industries are relying more on workers trained overseas. Companies are also focusing on increasing employment among under-represented groups, such as women, Indigenous Australians, and young people. Strategies to encourage women's participation include offering flexible hours and improving workplace culture.

There is growing recognition that workforce roles and structures need to be reconsidered to make the best use of available skills. Professional development programs, including training, mentoring, and career progression opportunities, are well established across industries. Some resources companies are also creating flexible roles to retain experienced older workers.

There are strong partnerships between employers and training organisations, with tailored programs designed to meet industry needs. These initiatives could be expanded further.

Workers increasingly value a good work-life balance. However, except for flexible options for older workers, many employers struggle to offer incentives that support this. Childcare is the most in-demand benefit but is in short supply. Employers consistently identified childcare as a major factor in attracting and keeping staff. The availability and quality of secondary education also influence workforce retention.

Some companies have recognised the importance of cooperation within communities. They are supporting shared training initiatives, preventing employee poaching between businesses, and investing in community amenities to improve living conditions for workers and their families.

For the health sector, it is clear that workforce incentives need to be tailored to individuals, considering their family needs, life stage, and career goals. While salary alone is not enough to attract workers to rural and remote areas, it must at least be competitive. The experience of the resources industry suggests that a 20% salary difference is necessary to attract professionals to regional areas. However, pay differences in the public health sector are currently small.

Regional allowances and additional payments must be updated to reflect the true cost of living in rural areas. The most pressing issue that needs to be addressed is the availability of affordable and high-quality housing.

Workforce roles should continue to be adapted to maximise the skills of available workers and provide fulfilling job opportunities. Flexible work arrangements that meet the needs of women and older workers will also be essential in improving workforce retention.

Health authorities should work closely with regional development organisations, local governments, education providers, and industry to create integrated workforce plans that address the needs of both employers and communities.

26

Improving Healthcare in Rural Australia: The Central West Single Practice Model[22]

Providing quality healthcare in rural and remote Australia comes with its fair share of challenges, especially when it comes to attracting and keeping skilled health professionals. Doctors, nurses, allied health workers, and support staff are essential for good healthcare, but many rural communities struggle to keep them around. This leads to service disruptions, hefty costs for temporary locum staff, and a lack of consistent care for patients.

To tackle this issue, Queensland introduced the Queensland Rural Generalist Pathway (QRGP) in 2005, a program designed to encourage and support medical graduates to take up jobs in rural areas. But bringing in more doctors alone isn't enough. Rural healthcare needs a well-organised system for managing services, funding, training, and quality of care. This is where the Central West Single Practice Model comes in, aiming to bring all these elements together to create a stronger, more efficient healthcare system in one of Queensland's largest rural health districts.

The Central West Health and Hospital Service (CWHHS) district spans a massive 385,000 square kilometres—around 22% of Queensland—but serves a small and widely dispersed population of just over 12,000. The number of residents doubles in winter as tourists flock to the region, adding extra strain to health services.

---

22. Derived from a paper given with Dr David Rimmer to the Rural Medical Conference, Adelaide, 2016.

The district includes a 31-bed acute hospital in Longreach, smaller hospitals in Barcaldine, Alpha, Blackall, and Winton, as well as general practices and community health services. With ongoing drought and economic pressures, making health services sustainable and reliable has been a key priority.

For many years, rural Queensland relied on the Medical Superintendent with Right of Private Practice (MSRPP) system, which was formalised in 1989. This model allowed doctors to work in public hospitals while running private practices, ensuring they had a stable income and broad service availability. However, by the early 2000s, fewer doctors were willing to take on these roles, leaving many rural towns without enough medical staff. The QRGP helped by training rural generalists with advanced skills so they could serve these communities more effectively. Even so, the separation between public hospitals and private general practices remained a challenge. When Longreach Hospital struggled with recruitment, the viability of its private general practice was also at risk, leading to increased reliance on locums and temporary fixes.

A Single Practice Model was trialled in Longreach as a solution. Initially, a private general practice was contracted to supply doctors to the hospital, but this proved unsustainable due to workforce shortages. By 2009, Queensland Country Practice (QCP) and health service leaders developed a more viable approach: the General Practice Management Company (GPMC). This new model allowed CWHHS to employ a shared workforce serving both the hospital and general practice, while the GPMC handled private practice operations. Over time, this setup was extended to other towns, ensuring continued medical services in communities where private general practices had struggled to survive.

Bringing public and private healthcare together under a single coordinated workforce helped address major challenges. Doctors could work across primary care and hospital settings, ensuring consistent and continuous care. A shared medical record system improved efficiency, reducing errors and enhancing chronic disease management. The model also made full use of the advanced skills of Rural Generalists, such as obstetrics, emergency medicine, and anaesthetics, reducing unnecessary transfers to larger hospitals.

Medical staff were deployed flexibly across different locations, with telehealth and digital records further improving service delivery. The financial sustainability of the model was strengthened by allowing the GPMC to handle business operations while CWHHS focused on clinical governance. This freed up doctors to concentrate on patient care rather than administrative tasks. Education and training were also built into the model, ensuring a steady pipeline of skilled professionals to sustain the workforce in the long term.

Since its introduction, the Single Practice Model has shown promising results. The number of full-time equivalent (FTE) doctors in the district rose from just five in 2012 to eighteen in 2016. The model reduced the reliance on locums, saving money that could be reinvested in healthcare services. Hospital activity increased, outpatient services moved into general practices, and telehealth usage doubled. Continuity of care improved, leading to fewer unnecessary hospital admissions and better management of chronic conditions. The work environment also became more attractive for doctors, improving retention and recruitment.

By integrating public and private services, eliminating competition for resources, and fostering collaboration, the Central West Single Practice Model is proving to be a practical and effective solution for rural healthcare. Its success highlights the importance of strong leadership, adaptability, creative problem-solving, and a commitment to training. As rural healthcare continues to face challenges, this model offers a roadmap for other regions looking to build a more stable, efficient, and patient-focused health system. The achievements in Central West Queensland could serve as inspiration for similar initiatives across Australia and beyond.

27

The challenge of Health Workforce Planning

The provision of high quality health care requires the availability of a well-trained, highly skilled workforce that is sufficient in number, capable of deployment to areas of high need and able to adapt and change in response to changing health care needs and changes in clinical and technical practice.

In responding to these requirements, the Australian health care system has faced some significant challenges. The country is vast, with a distributed population. Supply of the health workforce is faced with concentrations of demand in large population centres but significant and particular health care demands in relatively isolated centres. Health workforce supply to rural and remote communities, outer suburban areas and in support for Aboriginal and Torres Strait Islander communities has been a continuing challenge.

Australia has multiple responsible health authorities including the Commonwealth Government, State and Territory governments. Responsibilities are shared across public and private health care systems. Each authority has its own policies and priorities with respect to health care and in consequence, differential approaches to health workforce planning.

The required profile of the health workforce is changing as the population and the health profile of the community changes. An ageing population and one in which chronic conditions are more prevalent requires a different knowledge base for clinicians and greater flexibility in roles and deployment.

These factors contribute to a need for a coherent health workforce framework which can provide a basis for coordinated activity across health administrations, health education providers, professional associations, health employers and industrial bodies.

A number of initiatives have sought to address the challenges for health workforce planning. These have included:

Professional registration: The establishment of AHPRA has formalised the credentialing and registration of health professions and has introduced a level of knowledge about scale and distribution of health professionals' engagement;

Medical graduate numbers: The increase in the number of medical student places and increase in the number of medical schools has seen an increase in the overall number of medical graduates. The lack of growth in specialist training places however has meant that the full value of these increases has not been realised.

Impact of Rural Clinical Schools: The number of medical (and to some extent allied health) graduates who are choosing to practice, at least in the first instance in rural settings has increased as a direct impact of the development of rural clinical schools.

Increased numbers of Indigenous graduates and enhancement of Aboriginal Health Worker roles: There has been a slow but steady increase in the number of health care graduates from an Indigenous background, including in medicine.

Growth in interprofessional clinical education: The majority of medical and health sciences education programs now contain elements of inter-professional education. This may include shared initial years with later specialisation, common course elements and to a limited degree, shared field practicums. There continues to be a difficulty however in aligning the schedules of undergraduate programs so that students can participate in shared clinical placements.

Development of innovative vocational group categories: Some educational innovations have supported approaches to role delineation that transcend traditional vocational designations. Nurse Practitioner and Physician Assistant role are now supported through a number of institutions though they continue to face some professional and regulatory impediments.

Despite these developments however, there continue to be significant challenges facing health workforce planning, including rural health workforce planning. These include:

Mid-career attrition: Across the health professions, but particularly in nursing, there is a loss of personnel in mid-career. Workers undertake significant training and a number of years refining their skills and then leave their profession either for an extended period of time or permanently. This is most commonly attributed to a perception that they have reached the limits of their potential for professional development or frustration that the work context does not allow them to utilise the breadth or depth of their skills.

Changing clinical profiles: Complex co-morbidity is of the essence of contemporary health care. As the focus of health care has increasingly become upon the management of chronic and continuing conditions, the knowledge and skills required for practice increasingly span professional disciplines. Chronic disease management is of its nature multi-disciplinary and clinical practice in this area is increasingly inter-professional. Health workers are challenged to work collaboratively across disciplines and increasingly to work with a sheared knowledge and skills base.

Continuing rigidities in role demarcation: While the larger number of new graduates are trained at least partly in inter-disciplinary care, this is often not reflected in workplace organisation and in the construction of service models. There is a sense in which the potential created by increased role flexibility is not being realised because of the lack of a change orientation in health care management.

Rapidly changing knowledge and skills requirements: New technologies are entering health care systems at an increasing rate: remote sensors, robotics, genomics, stem cells, and artificial intelligence are becoming part of contemporary medical care. Medicines can now be combined with nanotechnologies and digital tools. 3D printing is being used to manufacture implants, and bioprinting is being used to modify organ transplantation. Precision medicine, which establishes links between individuals' biology and their diseases, promises to increase understanding of diseases and help better target treatments. Vast amounts of electronic data generated by health systems and by individuals, offer the prospect of improvement in all health system activities, including clinical care, population health, research and service development. The lag time between medical and technical innovation and its adoption in clinical practice is reducing markedly. Health workers are required to continually upgrade their knowledge in order to operate within best practice. The demands for the assimilation of new knowledge impacts across the education and workforce planning sectors in complex ways. It impacts upon course curricula and the requirements for continuing professional development. It creates a pressure towards increasing specialisation when the pressure within workplaces is towards generalisation.

Conflicting industrial and job profiles between jurisdictions; Employment structures within jurisdictions and approaches to workforce organisation vary markedly. In Queensland and NSW, the public sector workforce is employed directly by the State government. In Victoria, these employees are budget sector but are directly employed by health services. In some states there are standard contracts of employment while in others they vary. NSW nurses are employed with higher rates of pay but do not have nurse/patient ratios as are legislated in Victoria. In Queensland, Rural Generalist medical officers are guaranteed seniority within the Queensland public service but this option is not available in other states.

Absence of terminological consistency and shared discourse concerning planning: There are not common and accepted descriptions and ways of talking about workforce which are common across Australia. At a minimum there is a need for consistency of language and underlying concepts in workforce planning across the network of responsible planning and co-ordinating bodies.

Continuing deficiencies in workforce numbers and profile: Despite the progress made, there continue to be gaps in the number of health professionals available to service Indigenous communities and rural and remote communities. There is not the profile of health professionals, particularly with respect to allied health, that these communities require. The prevalence of chronic disease in these communities places considerable strain upon the existing health workforce.

Public/private tensions: The public and private health care systems compete for a limited pool of potential recruits from the health workforce. This is a distorted market which disadvantages parts of the service delivery sector. The public aged care system, for instance is at a considerable market disadvantage. The relatively recent development of *MyAgedCare* and the NDIS has brought about some restructuring of the market, particularly for allied health services. Increasing numbers of allied health professionals are choosing to become sole traders or go into private practice, with implications for the recruitment of public health care staff. A similar affect was created when clinical psychology became covered by the MBS.

Dominant Trends

A number of dominant trends are well recognised as impacting upon the provision of health care and health workforce and are expected to have a continuing and significant effect. These include:

- **Growth in chronic and complex care demand.** An increasing number of consumers of health care experience multiple co-morbid conditions or chronic disease. Their treatment requires interventions, over time, by multiple means in a variety of settings using the knowledge and skills of multiple vocational groups.
- **Changing technology.** Advances in medical technology and treatment protocols can have a significant impact upon the knowledge and skills requirements for health practitioners. Digital connectedness has the potential to enhance and support remote providers of health care.
- **Changing consumer expectations of care provision.** Consumers are increasingly expressing their views as to what services they should receive, where they will receive them and the ways in which they are provided. Increased consumer expectations also create additional demands upon health carers in the way they communicate with consumers and the way in which they support consumer preferences.
- **Preventive health.** An increased focus upon the prevention of illness and promoting the health of communities, including the prevention of and early intervention for infectious and chronic physical diseases and mental distress within communities, has implications for the profile of the health workforce with a greater emphasis upon educational and allied health resources. It has implications for the knowledge and skills requirements of the workforce.
- **Ageing.** An ageing population has particular care needs, often related to continuing care requirements and complex co-morbidities, and degenerative conditions such as dementia. It requires a multi-disciplinary workforce and an integrated care model. In many rural areas the clinical workforce is also

ageing, and organisations are struggling to replace clinicians as they retire or leave the workforce. The ageing of the community and the workforce, particularly in rural areas, are major issues for health workforce planning.
- **Developing service purchasing models.** New approaches to service purchasing in the aged care and disability sectors involves a movement away from service organisation based funding and towards consumer directed care. Amongst the implications of this for health workforce planning are increased employment in expanding disability and community aged care sectors, a developing private sector of sole trader and small business allied health providers, the emergence of new categories of care workers which are unregulated and a developing scope of practice and organisational uncertainty for health service providers that have provided services across the health, aged care and disability spectrum. These competing demands will impact upon health service delivery in more traditional settings, health workforce distribution efforts and the ability to plan for the appropriate capability and capacity to meet developing health care demands.

Systemic features of the health care system are structural elements of the way in which health care is organised which have implications for health workforce planning. Amongst these are:

- **Funding and purchasing arrangements.** Funding and purchasing arrangements reflect and support a two tiered separated set of health services nationally. Currently, health service funding arrangements do not enable integration of these tiers in the provision of health care for people with chronic and complex health conditions. The ability for health services to respond collaboratively to health risk factors in communities that contribute to a range of preventable chronic diseases and conditions is inhibited by historical funding arrangements. Innovative models of funding to redress some or all of these inhibiting factors are in place

and in development. Funding and purchasing arrangements do not facilitate systematic capacity to meet the range of health needs of communities with higher rates of risk factors and established chronic conditions. These communities are usually communities with high rates of socio-economic disadvantage, rural and remote communities, Aboriginal and Torres Strait Island communities and particular population groups. Funding and purchasing arrangements can inhibit the development of health workforce capacity to respond to these community needs.
- **Jurisdictional differences**. Separation of planning between levels of government and between care streams introduces barriers that affect engagement of health workforce in some geographic areas and some service streams. Jurisdictions have differing workforce needs due to geography and population, and approach this in different ways according to their resources and capability. Health workforce planning within jurisdictions should support collaborative work and strategies between and across jurisdictions to redress health workforce maldistribution; including through collaborative planning with tertiary institutions and professional bodies on health workforce education and training strategies to address unmet need.
- **Accreditation, Credentialing and Registration.** There is a variety of means by which professional education programs are accredited and health professionals are accredited to practice. 15 health professions are required to be registered under the National Registration and Accreditation Scheme. These arrangements have implications for the supply of health professionals, their scope of practice, the structure of service provision and the relationships between health professionals in clinical settings. Development of an adequate and effective health workforce that delivers the health workforce relevant to health profiles of diverse communities would be supported by accreditation, credentialing and registration provisions that promote flexible skills development and appropriate deployment of the health workforce to address unmet need.

In addition to the structural elements of health workforce organisation, a number of currently presenting challenges have been identified for health workforce planning. These include:

- **Information requirements.** All organisations involved in planning for the health workforce require access to information. This includes information about health needs so that the required health services and providers can be anticipated; information about demand for health care and for particular professional skills and capabilities; information about supply of health workforce including the specifics of local health organisation; and, information about the effectiveness of interventions to address health workforce needs.
- **Underserved populations.** Some communities in Australia do not have access to the health professionals required to meet their care needs. This is particularly the case for some rural and remote communities and there are serious deficits in services available to Aboriginal and Torres Strait Islanders. Providing for underserved populations goes beyond addressing distributional issues and includes matching of workforce resources to the specific cultural and service needs of hard to serve communities.
- **Maldistributions.** Access to health care services and to health care professionals is not equally distributed across Australia. There are distortions in the supply of primary care resources, including doctors, nurses and allied health professionals to the disadvantage of rural and remote communities.
- **Vocational and service relationships.** The evolving nature of contemporary health care requires flexibility in roles and multidisciplinary care which combines the skills of multiple professions in collaborative teams. This requires a balancing of care needs, negotiation between existing service roles and an examination over time of vocational requirements.
- **Succession planning.** As the current rural health workforce ages in profile and increasingly moves towards retirement ages, planning is required to replace that workforce and

to provide support and training for developing clinicians. This requires attention to supply of health professionals, the capacity to provide skilled supervision and personal and professional expectations of beginning practitioners particularly with respect to rural practice.
- **Alignment of education pathways.** Effective health workforce planning requires a level of alignment between workforce training and anticipated workforce demand, distribution of workforce training to areas of workforce need, the provision of post-graduate vocational training required to meet community health needs. Processes are required to ensure that trainee numbers meet anticipated demand and provide opportunities for people to undertake education and training in regional, rural and remote areas throughout the whole of their student years and to assist graduates to transition into long-term employment in areas of high need.
- **Specialism/generalism.** Health workforce planning , particularly in rural communities and in response to chronic and complex health care needs, has to consider the importance of generalist health care provision, at primary care, secondary care and tertiary care levels, as well as the expectations and aspirations of health care graduates for their careers and the scope of practice of health professionals as determined by credentialing and registration processes.

Principles

Health workforce planning principles to underpin and guide all planning processes provide for consistency and complementarity of the work of organisations that are engaged in planning for and facilitation of the health workforce of the future. The following principles have been derived from the literature and from a national consultation process. They reflect the desire of participants within the health workforce planning sector to have broad principles that address systemic and structural elements of health workforce planning nationally, regionally and locally. The principles that address these issues are:

Health workforce planning takes place collaboratively between governments, health care providers, education and training organisations and professional associations to meet shared priorities and agreed outcomes. Health workforce planners understand the workforce needs of other stakeholders and seek opportunities to generate shared goals, coordinated strategies and complimentary actions.

Planning is population health based and derived from the best available evidence. Health workforce planners seek to place individual planning issues in the context of community health needs assessments and an understanding of the social context of service provision.

Planning supports the distribution of the health workforce in such a way as to facilitate equivalent access to high quality care for all Australians. Maldistributions of workforce will occur for a variety of reasons. Health workforce planners understand why these exist and the levers which are available to influence distribution.

Planning ensures that the optimal use is made of available health workforce resources by supporting clinicians to exercise their full scope of practice. Health care workers generally have broad training and a scope of practice which can be adapted to a variety of contexts. Best use of resources supports a flexible and adaptive use of available workforce resources.

Planning provides workforce support for models of care in rural and remote areas that are effective in responding to the local needs and conditions. Continuing deficits in numbers and types of clinicians in rural areas may require that the way in which services are provided is reconsidered and alternative models of care are developed. Health workforce planning is attuned to the development of a workforce to support innovative approaches.

Planning contributes to health care services being culturally safe and respectful. Health workforce planning is concerned with the quality as well as the numbers of health care workers. An important aspect of quality is having an understanding of the cultural experiences and values of consumers and having appropriate knowledge, skills and attitudes to respond to these.

Planning engages with education provision to ensure that the workforce is skilled and competent and supported in continuing education to respond to changes in health care and community expectations. The intersection of the education and training system and the health workforce planning system is critical in order that the supply of health care workers is adequate and appropriate to health care needs.

Priorities

Health workforce planning encompasses ongoing monitoring and articulation of current and prospective workforce demand; the coordination of appropriate workforce supply through health professional education and training strategies; processes of recruitment and measures to support retention of the required workforce and strategies to ensure appropriate workforce deployment to provide equity in access to services. Ongoing evaluation of these measures is needed to provide for continuous improvement in response to changing health care needs and health technologies.

Health workforce planning priorities to support these activities and address current and anticipated health workforce challenges include:

> **Governance structures** support effective health workforce planning nationally, regionally or locally, across key players from relevant Commonwealth, State and Territory government agencies and other planning bodies and service providers.
>
> **Collaboration** between health, education, vocational training and regulatory authorities ensures a health workforce that has the knowledge and skills to meet the current and anticipated health needs for communities.

Clear roles and responsibilities for key stakeholders facilitate and support effective health workforce planning through strategic plans, initiatives and activities.

High quality evidence and information informs effective planning for health workforce decision making and development.

Local innovation in health workforce planning including new models of care further supports continual system improvements.

Enhancement through funding models, incentives and MBS rebates improves the provision of health care services to regional and rural communities.

Support for health professionals to work to their full scope of practice improves the recruitment and retention of the health care workforce and service delivery to local communities.

Multi-disciplinary integrated clinical models provide access to quality health care for the growing prevalence of chronic and complex diseases in the community.

Strengthened primary care services and providers particularly in regional and rural health areas.

Improved distribution of the medical, nursing and allied health workforce to underserved communities through incentive arrangements and other policy levers improves health outcomes.

Health workforce education and training supports equitable access to quality health care for the **needs of cultural groups**, particularly Aboriginal and Torres Strait Islander communities and consumers from CALD communities.

28

Place Management: An alternative approach to Public Administration[23]

In the early 21st century, a fresh approach to public sector governance called place management began to take shape. It emerged as a way to tackle complex, interconnected issues affecting local communities, particularly those doing it tough with economic and social disadvantage. The roots of this idea lie in urban and regional planning, but its real power comes from breaking down government silos and shifting the focus from bureaucratic outputs to real outcomes. Place management works by ensuring services and policies make practical sense on the ground, building public trust, and creating community development models that actually work.

The term "place" in place management isn't set in stone. It can mean a specific location, a natural resource system like a river catchment, or even any coherent system where different elements come together as a whole. Essentially, it's a flexible concept that can be expanded or shrunk depending on the circumstances. On the "management" side of things, place management is about giving authority to individuals or organisations to determine outcomes, set policies, and allocate resources for a specific place.

There's some debate about what place management actually is. Some say it's just a top-down government tool, while others argue it centralises control at the local level. Masters calls it "a concept in search of a definition," pointing out the confusion over whether it's

---

23. Material prepared with Claudia Trasancos for place management projects in the Hume Region.

about long-term reform or just a crisis response. The key concerns include uncertainty around what "place" actually means, who's in charge, how communities are involved, and what people expect from service delivery.

Despite this confusion, certain characteristics define place management. One key aspect is equity; ensuring that disadvantaged areas and groups receive the support they need. It recognises that not all people and places start on equal footing. Another important characteristic is accountability. A designated place manager is responsible for integrating policies and achieving tangible improvements in community wellbeing. Unlike traditional project management, which is about ticking boxes, place management is holistic and outcome-driven.

A major goal of place management is to make public services work better together. Many government programs operate separately, leading to inefficiencies and confusion. Place management coordinates and integrates service delivery so that programs complement rather than contradict each other. To do this effectively, governance needs to be flexible. Decision-making, funding, and accountability processes must adapt to fit local needs and involve the community in meaningful ways.

Mant describes place management as part of a broader shift in public sector governance. Traditionally, local government has focused on specific functions—like fixing roads—rather than broader outcomes, such as improving access to transport. This "silo" approach means services are often disconnected from what a community actually needs. The challenge is to restructure government so that resources are allocated based on real outcomes rather than rigid departmental budgets. As Latham points out, existing government structures make it difficult to reallocate public funds in ways that best serve local communities.

At its core, place management aims to bring government, businesses, and communities together to address issues at a local level. In Australia, it's been applied in different ways, including economic development initiatives, integrated planning projects, and efforts to tackle specific problems like unemployment and crime. Internationally, similar ideas have been trialled, particularly in the

UK, where the government has tried to combat social exclusion through coordinated, area-based policies. The Blair government's Neighbourhood Renewal Strategy, for example, aimed to improve conditions in the most deprived areas by ensuring key services like schools and healthcare met certain standards.

However, not all place-based policies have been successful. Research in Europe suggests that while these initiatives have improved service delivery in some cases, they often rely too much on individual champions rather than sustainable systems. Bureaucracy can also be a major stumbling block, with government schemes creating layers of red tape that slow down progress rather than streamlining solutions. There's also the issue of long-term sustainability—many programs start strong but fail to keep momentum once funding dries up.

In Australia, place-based approaches have a long history, dating back to post-war regional planning efforts and initiatives like the Whitlam government's Department of Urban and Regional Development. More recent efforts have focused on integrating social and economic policies at a local level. However, critics argue that government programs are still too fragmented, and that services are often rolled out without a coherent local strategy. A major challenge is ensuring government departments and agencies work together rather than in isolation.

For place management to work properly, it needs to be embedded within a broader framework. Walsh outlines a three-tiered approach: a statewide focus for program targeting, regional coordination to monitor and guide efforts, and local place management for hands-on intervention. This layered approach ensures that problems are tackled at the right scale while avoiding duplication and inefficiency.

One of the biggest hurdles to place management is balancing state-wide equity with local needs. Governments are responsible for distributing resources fairly across all communities, but place management demands flexibility to address specific local issues. This tension can make it difficult to get the right level of funding and authority to the people who need it most. Some argue that the solution lies in better data-driven planning, where funding is allocated based on clear, evidence-based assessments of local needs.

Victoria's approach to place management has been shaped by its broader public administration model, which focuses on purchasing services based on outputs. While this system aims for efficiency, it can make it harder to deliver holistic, community-focused services. The rigid nature of output-based funding means services are often fragmented, rather than coordinated in a way that makes sense for local communities. To fully embrace place management, the government would need to rethink how it structures funding and service delivery.

The future of place management in Australia depends on how well governments can integrate local and regional planning efforts. If done right, it has the potential to create stronger, more resilient communities by tailoring services to local needs and breaking down bureaucratic barriers. However, without genuine collaboration between government, business, and the community, there's a risk that it becomes just another layer of red tape rather than a meaningful change to the way public services are delivered. The key is ensuring that place management is driven by local priorities, not just administrative convenience, so that it actually makes a difference on the ground.

29

Managing for Place: Some Challenges Facing Human Services Management[24]

Place Management has developed as a key policy goal of Government in Victoria and is proposed as an alternative paradigm for public sector management in the State. This paper will examine some aspects of its application to the administration of Health, Community Services and Housing Programs, seek to identify some key elements of its application, and identify some of the challenges facing the Department of Human Services in its implementation.

Definitional Issues

The discourse on place-based management features a number of inter-related concepts with some definitional impression. For the purpose of this paper, key concepts are utilised in the following way:

> **Place-based service management** refers to the administration of service activity utilising a locational reference. This may be contrasted with service organisation based upon functional (e.g. housing, health etc.), categorical (e.g. youth, disability etc.), a program (e.g. service activity) disjunctions. The concept carries with it assumptions about the added value of citizen participation in service decision making.

---

24. Policy proposal circulated within the Department of Human Services 2004.

Social Capital as a concept, derives from the work in the late 1970s by Bronfenbrenner and generalised to the broader social context by Robert Putnam and others. It asserts that social wellbeing may be enhanced by the promotion of social connectedness, and conversely, that the absence of social capital (i.e. the breakdown of social connectedness) is a significant factor in societal dysfunction. The concept is notoriously difficult to operationalise. How might levels of social capital be measured for instance. Also, many commentators remark on the "dark side" of social connectedness i.e. it may be exclusive as well as inclusive and may be equally present in anti-social groups as socially supportive groups.

Capacity Building derives from the public health literature and refers to the enhanced capacity which may be created by organisational alliances of various forms. It asserts that organisations working together are able to achieve more than where they are working separately; that the whole is greater than the sum of the parts. The term has come to be applied very loosely to any activity, which enhances sustainable output. When applied to communities as distinct from organisations, it has less definitional clarity.

Community Development refers to the enhancement of base level social organisation through the promotion of participation by individuals and groups in decisions and processes that effect their wellbeing. It had its origins in the social programs and urban redevelopment activities of the late 1960s but has been in disfavour during the period in which public administration has been principally focused upon service outputs rather than social processes. It has come to be seen less as a goal than as an approach i.e. service development utilising a community development approach would seek to engage citizens in defining service requirements.

Joined-up Government has been developed as an administrative strategy by the Blair government in Britain. It argues that the traditional functional disjunctions utilised in public administration undervalue the inter-connectedness of administrative decisions and activities. Joined-up government as an approach has tended to promote non-traditional structures, which force linkages between clients and public sector organisation and mediating structures, which focus upon end-user groups.

Background

The Predecessor organisations of DHS have had a history of locationally oriented public administration. This is reflected in the regionalisation of their service arrangements. The principle benefits of regionalisation were seen to be effective management control through devolved decision making, enhanced decision quality through access to local knowledge, and integration of services within a defined context. The Social Welfare Department/Community Welfare Services Department regionalised its operations in the late 1970s and building upon the Australian Assistance Plan, developed the Family and Community Program (FACS) to provide a strong community interface with Departmental operations. The Health Department regionalised in the mid-1980s. The original Health regionalisation plan proposed nine regions which would themselves be the Department's programs. For a brief period in the late 1980s, District Health Councils were seen as a means by which the Health Department might engage with Community interests.

The machinery of government changes of 1985 which created a community services department signalled the beginning of a change in focus, in that while children's services and disability services were integrated within a regional framework, the principle concern was the realignment of the functional domains of Departments to reflect a community services rather than a health orientation within these programs.

The Department of Health and Community Services was created following the 1992 election of the Kennett government. DHS was created with the amalgamation of Housing in 1995. Theoretically this provided the basis for a strong integration of services on a localised basis. The promise of an integrated Human Services Department has, however, never been realised. Amongst the factors which have contributed to this are; the preference of the then Secretary for "clear product lines"; the tendency of the Health function to disaggregate; the failure to properly integrate Housing within the wider Department; and the emergence of output based purchasing as the dominant paradigm of public administration during the 1990s.

The dominant paradigm of public administration during the 1990s was based upon the operation of quasi markets and output based funding. This paradigm drove significant productivity improvements, particularly in health service provision, but was accompanied by some significant negative service system impacts. The focus upon service outputs ignored the relationship between these outputs and undervalued the infrastructure required to produce them. At its worst, the tendering methodology which accompanied the output based purchasing system, awarded contracts for service provision on a price competitive basis, without regard to the community connectedness of the provider, or the required complimentary of service outputs.

The Department's functions have seen an inexorable drift of authority and responsibility to the centre over the past decade. This is explicable in a public administration system in which accountability (particularly by volume and price) is given priority over responsiveness. This tendency has continued despite the change of government in 1999. While there has been some movement towards enhanced flexibility and responsiveness in administrative practice e.g. relaxation of resource allocation business rules, simplification of service agreements, re-emphasis upon partnering, and the block funding of small rural hospitals, the inflexible specification of funding to an activity level has if anything increased over the past three years.

A number of structural decisions actively militate against a strong place-based approach to the Department's responsibilities. The transfer of acute budgets to the centre and the centralisation of responsibility for metropolitan acute health, and the amalgamation of metropolitan regions are principle in this. Difficulties have been created in integrating acute and non-acute health services in the metropolitan area, and metropolitan regions have ceased to represent communities of interest that could be used for services integration purposes. The proposed amalgamation of Western and Northern Regions is a policy absurdity in the context of government intent around integration by place.

Place-based management should not be seen as being exhausted by regional service delivery arrangements however integrated. It is clear that government has an expectation that services will be locally responsive and well-integrated **and** that government agencies will have integrated their approaches, **and** that there will be significant citizen participation in the implementation of that.

A Typology of place-based initiatives

There is currently a range of activities taking place within the Department and some programmatically established and some exploratory, which might be seen as fitting within a place-management rubric An inexhaustive description follows:

Project based exemplars: e.g. Department of Victorian Communities Community Building Initiatives.

These projects combine grass root initiatives with the potential for whole of state government agency support, and in some cases, Local Government engagement. Their principle advantage is in the demonstration of alternative collaborative ways of acting on the part of government agencies, with respect to local initiatives. They are limited however, by the fact that they are idiosyncratic projects with limited generalisability; have some lack of consensus about purpose between government and sponsor organisations; and the fact that they are concerned with marginal activity, rather than the core activities of government. They offer limited possibilities in modelling an alternative paradigm of public administration.

Issues based initiatives: Regional Domestic Violence Initiatives, Regional Disaster Management Initiatives, School retention for high-needs adolescents

Many issues at a local and regional level require cross functional approaches, particularly between DHS, Education and Justice. There are a variety of usually ad hoc planning and project management arrangements which have been established to deal either with pressing issues or issues identified as of major concern to the agencies involved. Their value lies in their strong local character i.e. dealing with the specifics of a local problem, and a shared commitment across agencies to flexibility and mutual problem solving. A limitation is their ad hoc nature and the fact that the strong inter-agency linkages involved do not always carry over into other areas of activity.

The increasing significance for all agencies of emergency management has contributed to the issue becoming a more sustained basis for inter-agency locality based collaboration. The recent example for the 2003 Alpine Bushfires saw the establishment of more formal interagency and non-government organisation co-coordinative arrangements, which managed the recovery exercise.

Local Government based strategies approaches: Municipal Public Health Plans, Municipal Child Development Plan

Local Government is a logical basis for integrated human services planning and place management. At least theoretically, Local Government provides an established governance and accountability structure with strong engagement with service users. While the level of engagement of Local Government with Human Services is variable, as is the effectiveness of its consultative mechanisms, recent years has seen an increased interest and sophistication in its involvement. Particularly where there is a statutory requirement that plans exist, there is a strong basis for engagement. Forward looking municipalities have taken a perspective on their public health responsibilities which is much broader than environmental health and surveillance activities, and in some cases, they have articulated their public health plans with PCP Community Service plans.

Program/Area based service co-ordination: Primary Care Partnership (PCP), Best Start, Small Rural Hospital Funding

This approach seeks to integrate a defined range of activities on an area or catchment basis. As such, it moves away from a service output, or single agency focus, and offers the potential for improved responsiveness to local conditions. At their best PCP's have articulated the relationship between Municipal Public Health Plans, and their own Community Services Plans.

PCPs as a mechanism for place based management offer some distinct possibilities. They have been hampered however by their origins in a failed service aggregation strategy, the over-specification of their outputs in the early stages of their development, and the fact that they have been variably adopted by major stakeholders such as hospitals and Local Government. The major limitation upon PCPs as a place management strategy is their narrowness of focus upon primary health care, and within this, the fact that they are unable to systemically link GPs as the major providers of primary health care.

Primary Care Partnerships are concerned principally with relationships internal to the functional responsibilities of Human Services, though, to the extent that they are able to engage with general practice, and Commonwealth funded aged care, relationships with Commonwealth agencies could become important.

Best Start in concerned to provide locationally based solutions to service co-ordination issues for children in the 0 to 8 age range. They have intended to be multi-systemic with principle relationships being between Human Services, Education and Local Government. They have utilised strategies for community engagement principally through Local Government and service agencies, but to the extent that they have initiated health promotion activities, have also established some broader basis for community consultation and engagement.

The Small Hospitals Funding initiative provides a degree of flexibility in resource deployment for health services of a particular size. This should allow greater responsiveness by health services to locally specific needs. It builds upon the success of the Multi-purpose Services program and the lessons from Health Streams initiatives. Limitations upon this as a place-based management initiative stem from the fact that all health services within given communities are not necessarily provided by the designated health services (e.g. HACC services), and the fact that the Commonwealth is not a participant. Aged Care, funded by the Commonwealth, represents a major component of the funding of these organisations.

Also, the health care needs and service provision requirements of rural communities are critically related to sub-regional provision through Group B referral hospitals. This initiative does not provide a basis for their integration.

Population Cohort specific initiatives – COAG Indigenous Trial

Area based initiatives may be defined by an identified population cohort such as an indigenous community, young people in a distinct area etc. A distinguishing feature of these approaches is that they may seek to be multi systemic, or whole of government in their strategies. Thus, the Shepparton COAG trial engages multiple Departments of both the Victorian and Commonwealth Governments with strategies that span major sectors of activity.

The COAG trial is multi-systemic in that it links all Victorian Government Department and Commonwealth Departments and has endorsement at the highest levels within both governments. It seeks to negotiate with the Indigenous community through a governance structure which reflects the complexity of the community and has developed a range of strategic responses to issues identified by that governance structure. It proposes a structure for co-ordinating cross functional government administrative activity.

Possible limitations of this approach relate to the fragility of newly generated community governance structures and a possible failure to recognise both the strengths and vulnerabilities in existing inter-organisational relationships. New approaches need to acknowledge the legacy of earlier arrangements. A key issue with this approach concerns the relationship between cohort based service initiatives and mainstream services. The capacity to address key strategic issues for indigenous and other cohorts through parallel administrative arrangements, run the risk of failing to engage those services which continues to be managed through mainstream structures.

Local Area Service Integration: Neighbourhood Renewal

Neighbourhood Renewal represents the most significant level of commitment to place-based management by DHS. It has provided a focus upon high need public housing estates, which not surprisingly, have high concentrations of users of other Departmental programs.

These initiatives are significant in that they have made possible a large commitment of additional resources (usually in the form of housing upgrades and replacement), and they have been approached flexibly, with renewal strategies being determined locally. They have required a strong local engagement with consumers, who have tended to have a determinative influence upon strategy.

Intersectional collaboration is a corner stone of neighbourhood renewal, with there being strong participation of Local Government and other agencies, particularly Education and Justice; though this has not generally entailed the contribution of resources. Inter-agency collaboration has been strongest where it has been mandated through the La Trobe Valley Ministerial Taskforce.

The most significant limitation upon Neighbourhood Renewal as a place management strategy has been the tendency for it to be treated within the Department as a housing initiative. Very little in the way of additional resource has been provided from non-housing programs, except where the renewal area is co-extensive with a program based initiative. Also, within Housing itself, neighbourhood renewal has tended to be a marginal activity, having little impact upon the highly centralised planning, resource allocation and asset management practices of that Division. If Neighbourhood Renewal is to realise its potential as a place-management strategy it needs to become mainstream to the Housing program and change the way Housing is transacted relative to other Department programs.

Whole of Government Strategic Implementation: The Seymour Inter-agency Project

Social Development priorities for the State of Victoria are established through the Growing Victoria Together strategy. The specific strategies that it proposes impact differentially upon communities and are variously affected by agencies of government. It is possible to analyse these strategies, establishing a matrix of possible contribution by a range of agencies. The task is then to identify a number of core activities which require multiple agency contributions, and to manage them as inter-agency projects.

The advantages associated with this approach are that it is more clearly driven strategically rather than opportunistically. It allows for a governance process which involves Local Government and all relevant agencies. Also, it has the potential to affect more radically the way in which agencies undertake their core business.

Limitations are that it is not immediately clear what mechanisms should or could be utilised for community engagement, except those provided indirectly by local government. Also the breadth of scope would require that a relatively small number of core projects would be identified. This may lead to the marginalisation of those activities.

Comprehensive Service Integration: The Wodonga Place-management Project

DHS is responsible for a broad range of government activity. Within the portfolio there is a capacity for comprehensive integration of service planning and management on an area or place basis. To do so requires an integration of existing program based planning, and a revision of purchasing frameworks away from unit purchasing.

The past three years have seen an explosion in program focused planning, much of which is at a subregional, or could be, at a sub-regional level. Municipal Public Health Plans, PCP Community Service Plans, Area Mental Health plans, drug services plans, acute health services plans, relate to the same populations and frequently deal with overlapping concerns. They are poorly articulated however and are not linked by a developed population health framework, or an integrated purchasing framework.

Developing such an approach would realise the benefit of having an integrated Human Services Department and is perhaps the primary rationale for doing so. Moreover, the task is not a particularly difficult one, since in most areas of Departmental activity, sub-regional plans are available or possible. There are significant impediments however, both with respect to Central Agency accountability and internal Departmental rigidities.

This approach would result in the purchasing by the Region of a sub-regional health/community services/housing plan with specified total outputs with agreed degrees of freedom for variations, articulated roles for providers and articulated service relationships. Having a clear framework for the integration of

Departmental functions at a sub-regional level would make possible the identification of key strategic linkages with other agencies.

Each of the above approaches to place based management makes a significant contribution in its own right. They be mapped with respect to a number of key variables. **Scope** is concerned with the range of activities which is the concern of the initiative. **Scale** refers to the catchment, geographic unit of attention or population cohort which is the focus of activity. **Governance** refers to the mechanism for direction of the activity. **Planning framework** refers type and nature of the formal specification of service outputs. **Community Engagement** refers to the mechanism for consumer/citizen participation in planning delivery or managing the activity, and **Purchasing Framework** refers to the mechanism developed for financial accountability.

Some propositions

DHS is uniquely placed to pursue a place-based management approach. It has a developed de-centralised structure, strong local knowledge, and well established relationships with local and regional services, community organisations and government agencies. Moreover, it is responsible for a significant component of all government activity delivered at the local and regional level. There are however significant inhibitors, principally in the rigidity of output group structures and the central tendency of decision making, especially with respect to resource allocation.

The style and type of community engagement required to support these initiatives requires consideration. The focus of the Departments place management activities should be principally upon middle order social infrastructure rather than local community development. A principle role of the Department in this regard is the development and maintenance of integrated sustainable social infrastructure which is closely aligned with presenting community expectations and service requirements. The Department is too far removed from the action to be directly involved in primary level community development. It is appropriate however that the Department have requirements of the agencies it funds, that they have established mechanisms for community engagement and that mechanisms be developed which promote engagement across program boundaries. Local Government may be of significance in this. An exception may be where the Department has a direct relationship with service areas, for instance, a public housing estates facing redevelopment.

Community engagement at a higher level of strategic decision making would be possible, although this should probably span government agencies. If this were to be the case it would act at such a level of generality and have to process such a significant level of detail, as to risk being ineffectual or overwhelmed. Also, current regional boundaries of all government agencies encompass large areas which are incomprehensible from a citizen perspective. This requires further consideration.

It is tempting to focus place management initiatives upon disadvantage since it is clear that communities and localities in which there is a high prevalence of disadvantage may gain most from multi-systemic interventions. It needs to be kept in mind however, that the bulk of the Department's services are accessed by everyone in the community at some stage in their life. By preference, place management strategies should be 'whole of community' a 'whole of cohort' focused.

The great strength of the Victorian Health and Community Services system is in service management. In fact, few jurisdictions manage as well for price, volume or quality. Its great weakness is its absence of a population health context or imperative. While most service planning has a well-developed socio-demographic profile, this seldom has a significant impact upon purchasing decisions. The Department has at its disposal a great wealth of epidemiological data. This is sometimes used for program design purposed, but seldom, if ever, used for planning and resource allocation. A place based management approach would assume an enhanced population health capacity.

The typology of place management approaches outlined above form a hierarchy from least to most systemic in their impact. A goal of the Department with respect to place based management should seek to pilot a number of initiatives at the higher end of the table.

These initiatives will require effective community consultative arrangements, a developed population health and planning framework, and collaboration with other government Departments. These higher end initiatives provide a basis for systemic reform.

Local Government provides a strong potential platform, and partner for DHS in the development of place-based initiatives. Municipal Public Health Planning should be more well supported and should be given a broader mandate and focus, with a view to it becoming a basis of place management within the Department.

The development of planning frameworks which link the range of Departmental activities and create the opportunity for inter-sectorial connection, require the development of alternatives to unit purchasing. An alternative purchasing framework must however enable a continuing capacity to manage to the other policy dimensions referred to above.

Central Agencies have already approved a capacity for Departments to transfer resources across Output Groups. This flexibility should be vested at the regional level to allow enhanced responsiveness to local issues.

30

Tools for Change: The Intellectual Disability Services Act 1986[25]

The *Intellectually Disabled Persons' Services Act 1986* marked a turning point in the provision of services for individuals with intellectual disabilities in Victoria. Emerging from an era of activism that had begun with the separation of the Mental Retardation Division from the Mental Health Division within the Health Commission, the Act was unapologetically reformist. Its purpose, as stated in the opening section, was clear: "to reform the law relating to services for disabled persons" (*IDPS Act*, 1986). This was the first Australian legislation to explicitly differentiate intellectual disability from mental illness, addressing long-standing fragmentation, lack of coordination, and inadequate resourcing in service delivery.

The Act established a comprehensive framework of principles and objectives to guide service provision. Section 5 outlined 14 principles, asserting the rights of intellectually disabled individuals to equal access, equal opportunity, and the benefits of normalisation. Central to these principles was the requirement that any restriction on a person's rights or opportunities should be the least restrictive option available. These ideals were reinforced elsewhere in the Act, where specific guidelines were set for the provision of services, all grounded in a commitment to dignity, worth, human rights, and the full potential of intellectually disabled people.

This legislative ambition translated into 22 specific objectives. These objectives sought to transform service planning, expand

---

25. Extract from Journal of Law and Social Work, Spring and Fall, 2000.

access to generic services, promote individualised care, and integrate individuals into the community. Particular emphasis was placed on moving residents of institutions into community-based accommodation, supported by high-quality care and developmental programming. The Act underscored the need to limit institutional admissions, ensuring such decisions were justified only when they would enhance the person's independence, avoid harm, and remain the least restrictive option.

The Act also defined intellectual disability for the first time in Victorian law, establishing criteria for eligibility. Intellectual disability was described as "a significant sub-average general intellectual functioning existing concurrently with deficits in adaptive behaviour and manifested during the developmental period." While this definition provided a framework for service eligibility, its lack of clarity led to legal challenges and confusion about what eligibility actually guaranteed. Some interpreted eligibility as an automatic entitlement to services, whereas the government argued it merely established prerequisites for access. This distinction became a source of contention, especially as transitional provisions conferred eligibility on many institutional residents whose diagnoses were ambiguous, including those with dual diagnoses of intellectual disability and mental illness.

Case planning emerged as a central element of the Act, with General Service Plans (GSPs) introduced as tools to specify areas of need and outline strategies for support. All eligible clients, including those receiving services prior to the Act, were entitled to a GSP. These plans were to be reviewed annually for institutional residents and every five years for community-based clients. GSPs represented a significant step toward coordinated service delivery, with the aim of fostering inter-agency collaboration and consistent case management. However, the practical implementation of GSPs faced significant challenges. Data collection systems were insufficiently developed, and the quality of information gathered was often poor. By 1991, efforts to create an intellectual disability services information system based on case planning had been abandoned in favour of a broader approach integrating other client service functions.

Accountability and oversight were fundamental to the Act's vision. The Intellectual Disability Review Panel (IDRP) was established to review critical decisions, including eligibility determinations, institutional admissions, and the use of restraint or seclusion. The IDRP scrutinised practices that were prevalent in institutional settings, such as chemical restraint and seclusion, and its investigations often brought these issues to public attention. Community Visitors were another key mechanism introduced under the Act. Appointed to inspect residential facilities and community accommodations, they reported annually to the Minister, with their findings tabled in Parliament. Community Visitors played a pivotal role in exposing substandard conditions in institutions such as Caloola and Aradale, prompting inquiries and reforms.

Despite its transformative ambitions, the Act revealed tensions between the principles it articulated and the realities of its implementation. The emphasis on integrating intellectually disabled individuals into generic services often clashed with the limited influence the administering department had over sectors such as education and legal services. Additionally, the principles outlined in the Act, while intended to confer general rights, were not legally enforceable. The only enforceable individual rights were the entitlement to a GSP and the ability to seek review of certain decisions.

The Act was also shaped by the political and economic context of its time. While funding for intellectual disability services increased between 1988 and 1991, these gains were largely driven by public concern over institutional conditions and specific projects, such as the closure of Caloola. Systemic change and expansion, as envisioned by the Act's architects, proved elusive. Budget constraints and administrative limitations often overshadowed the Act's broader goals, with growth in services focusing narrowly on addressing immediate crises rather than fostering long-term reform.

The legislation also faced criticism for its approach to casework services. The mandatory eligibility assessments and case planning processes introduced by the Act did not guarantee additional services, leading to frustrations among clients and families. Unlike similar legislation in the United States, the *IDPS Act* lacked constitutional authority and relied on administrative mechanisms to enforce rights. This created a gap between the Act's aspirational principles and its practical outcomes.

Nevertheless, the *IDPS Act* played a critical role in advancing public understanding of intellectual disability and the need for reform. The establishment of the IDRP and Community Visitors introduced unprecedented transparency and accountability, exposing institutional practices and prompting changes that would have been unlikely without such scrutiny. Reports from Community Visitors were instrumental in highlighting abuses and inadequacies, such as those uncovered at Caloola and Aradale, and in galvanising public and political support for reform.

In many ways, the Act embodied the tensions inherent in attempting to balance individual rights with administrative and regulatory responsibilities. While it sought to expand the government's role in supporting intellectually disabled individuals, it also revealed the complexities of building a service system that was both comprehensive and person-centred. The Act's legacy lies not only in its immediate impact on service delivery but also in its role as a catalyst for ongoing debate and reform, highlighting both the progress made and the challenges that remain in ensuring the rights and dignity of intellectually disabled people.

31

Promoting Science Careers in Health[26]

Studying science forms the foundation for many careers in health. Most health-related courses include science subjects, making a strong grounding in science from school essential. Developing an interest in science from an early age, ideally beginning in primary school, helps set the stage for later studies in health and medical fields. A review of international research explored ways to encourage school students to take up science, aiming to increase their participation in health-related education and training later on.

Governments worldwide recognise the importance of promoting science education, and similar challenges have emerged across countries. There is a strong industry demand for workers with scientific and mathematical skills, yet a shortage of skilled professionals in health and other science-related fields. The prioritisation of science teaching varies across primary schools, and many primary school teachers have different levels of confidence and knowledge in science subjects. Gender imbalances in science study persist, and there is a continued shortage of qualified science teachers.

Several factors contribute to the decline in students choosing science at secondary school. Parental attitudes and gender differences influence career encouragement. There is also a lack of trained and skilled teachers in subjects such as mathematics, physics, and chemistry, along with inconsistencies in the quality and availability of instructional materials. The way science is taught

---

26. Paper prepared for the Commonwealth Department of Health and Ageing, 2012.

plays a significant role, as research suggests the need for more hands-on, problem-solving approaches that connect science to real-world issues. Instead of focusing solely on science content, teaching should develop critical thinking skills and engage students through experimentation and inquiry-based learning.

To address this, various international strategies have been successfully implemented to increase interest in science and health careers. Coordinated national policies that integrate multiple initiatives have shown promise, along with increased funding for science education at all levels. Encouraging greater student engagement in science, providing incentives for students to study science subjects, and training and upskilling teachers have also contributed to positive outcomes. Supporting scientific societies, facilitating interactions between students and professional scientists, and expanding access to online learning resources and career guidance are additional ways to foster interest in science fields. Countries such as Japan and Taiwan have introduced specialist science-focused high schools, while many nations have reviewed and revised their school science curriculums to better align with industry needs and make science more engaging for students.

Identifying and supporting talented students early on has proven effective, particularly through programs aimed at increasing participation in health professions among underrepresented groups. Corporate investment in science education has also played a role, with initiatives such as scholarships, summer camps, and hands-on learning opportunities providing students with exposure to real-world science careers. Government and industry outreach into schools has further strengthened science education by supporting teachers, providing access to expert scientists, and recognising student achievements.

Encouraging partnerships between schools, universities, and the health sector can expose students to health professionals and create structured career pathways. Promoting science education is a key strategy in encouraging young people to consider health careers. Engaging children in health-related science learning from an early age, developing teaching materials that connect science education with real-world health applications, and ensuring teachers stay up to date with developments in health sciences are crucial steps. Increasing outreach programs that involve health professionals and offering hands-on, applied science options in schools can also provide students with valuable insight into the field.

International experiences suggest that defining career pathways early helps students work towards their future professions from secondary school. Collaboration between schools, vocational and tertiary institutions, industry organisations, universities, and employers plays a crucial role in supporting work experience, vocational education, and structured career pathways within the health sector. Exposure to real scientists has been identified as one of the most powerful influences on students choosing science careers. Expanding this to include interactions with health professionals could follow the model of Australia's 1980s "Tradeswomen on the Move" program, which successfully increased female participation in non-traditional trades. By showcasing the diverse and stimulating career opportunities in health sciences, more students may be encouraged to pursue these fields.

The use of technology should also be embraced to support science education, with the development of online learning tools, multimedia resources, national competitions, and interactive study forums in science and health fields. Efforts should focus on increasing participation in health careers among underrepresented groups, including Indigenous students and those in rural areas. Expanding existing initiatives, such as career pathway programs, literacy support, and mentoring opportunities, will help create a more diverse representation in the health workforce. Promoting and supporting health science careers for women remains a key priority, and international research highlights the value of long-term collaborations between schools and universities. By fostering these partnerships, Australia can move beyond fragmented efforts and establish sustainable, impactful programs that will shape a skilled and diverse health science workforce for the future.

32

Hospitals of the Future

Healthcare in Australia is changing rapidly as social, economic, and technological advancements reshape the way medical services are delivered. With growing knowledge in medical and social sciences, along with improved technology, healthcare is becoming more personalised and better suited to individual needs. However, these improvements come with increasing costs, and budget constraints limit what can be provided. The recent global pandemic has added another layer of complexity, with its lasting impacts on public health measures and community attitudes yet to be fully understood.

Hospitals have traditionally been the backbone of healthcare, offering critical care, housing expert medical knowledge, and serving as hubs for research and learning. However, their role is evolving. The idea of the "Hospital of the Future" is gaining attention, with healthcare shifting from simply treating illnesses to actively promoting health and wellbeing. This includes preventive care, rehabilitation, and lifestyle support. There is also a greater emphasis on achieving better clinical outcomes, aided by technology that improves precision and reduces errors. Hospitals are now seen as just one part of a broader healthcare network that includes GPs, pharmacies, rehabilitation centres, and community health services.

Patients today are more informed and want to be involved in their healthcare decisions. At the same time, there is growing focus on value and accountability in healthcare. Future hospitals are likely to focus on specialised, high-value services such as complex surgeries and intensive care while working in closer partnership with community-based healthcare providers. Digital connectivity, automation, patient-focused care, data-driven decision-making, and teamwork across different healthcare disciplines will define these hospitals.

The financial side of healthcare is also shifting. There is a move towards rewarding healthcare providers for keeping patients healthy, rather than just treating them when they become unwell. Telehealth, which grew significantly during the pandemic, has shown the potential of remote care. Models such as hospital-at-home, where medical professionals use telehealth and home visits to provide treatment, are becoming more common.

Alternatives to traditional hospital care are gaining momentum, particularly those that focus on community-based, team-based, and technology-supported approaches. Many of these models aim to integrate health and social care, provide outreach services, and ensure care is centred around the person. Instead of making hospitals the focal point, there is a push to bring care into local communities and homes, recognising that factors like housing, income, and education play a major role in health outcomes.

Public hospitals have typically been structured around specialisations, such as emergency care, surgery, and medical wards. However, an alternative model is based on place-based care, where services are designed around the needs of a specific community rather than just treating conditions in isolation. Research has shown that socio-economic factors strongly influence hospital use. People from lower-income backgrounds are more likely to be hospitalised for preventable conditions such as asthma, heart failure, and diabetes. By addressing these broader social factors, healthcare providers can reduce unnecessary hospital visits and improve overall community health.

Programs that integrate housing and healthcare have shown promising results, particularly for people with complex needs. For example, co-locating healthcare services within public housing developments allows for early intervention and more holistic support. While some studies suggest that living in public housing can sometimes have negative health effects, proactive healthcare programs can help mitigate these risks and improve wellbeing.

A key part of emerging healthcare models is the use of multidisciplinary teams. These teams bring together doctors, case managers, social workers, and mental health professionals to provide coordinated, comprehensive care. This approach is especially important for people with complex medical and social needs. Research has shown that programs involving multidisciplinary teams can reduce emergency visits and hospital admissions. Some research suggests that multidisciplinary approaches do not always lead to fewer hospital admissions, though they may improve quality of life. Partnerships between hospitals and community organisations can help strengthen these efforts, ensuring patients receive the right care at the right time.

Another major shift in healthcare delivery is the expansion of home-based and outreach services. Traditionally, patients have had to travel to outpatient clinics for follow-up care. However, newer models, such as hospital-at-home, allow people to receive acute care in their own homes. These services have been associated with high patient satisfaction and cost-effectiveness. While home-based care is well recognised in some countries, its adoption in Australia remains limited. Expanding these services will require changes to how healthcare is delivered, with greater investment in mobile healthcare teams and digital health tools.

Mental health services have long embraced community-based care, with mobile support teams providing treatment outside of hospitals. Research shows that people with serious mental illness benefit from supported housing and outreach case management. Programs that integrate health and social services have been shown to improve housing stability and reduce hospital admissions.

Palliative care is another area where home-based models are proving effective. Studies indicate that home-based end-of-life care allows more people to pass away at home, which is often their preference, while also reducing hospital costs. Expanding these services will require more investment in home healthcare teams and support for families.

Integrated and patient-centred care is at the heart of many of these innovations. The goal is to ensure that people receive seamless, coordinated care across different healthcare settings. Successful models of integrated care focus on teamwork, data-driven decision-making, and patient-centred treatment. Research suggests that integrated care improves patient satisfaction and access to services, though its impact on overall healthcare costs is still being studied.

Technology will play a crucial role in the future of healthcare. Smart hospitals will be part of a connected system that integrates digital health records, remote monitoring, and real-time data sharing. This will help ensure patients receive consistent, high-quality care no matter where they are. Telehealth has already proven its value, particularly during the pandemic, and will continue to be a key feature of modern healthcare.

For community hospitals, using technology effectively will be essential. Mobile outreach teams, electronic data exchange, smart clinical tools, and comprehensive digital records will support efficient and effective care. Ensuring data security and patient privacy will be vital as these systems expand.

The transformation of hospitals and healthcare services reflects a broader move towards more personalised, efficient, and community-focused care. A place-based, team-based approach designed around the needs of the local community can improve health outcomes and reduce avoidable hospital attendances and admissions. However, making this model work will require careful planning, clear service priorities, and sustainable funding.

By rethinking how healthcare is delivered, embracing technology, and prioritising integration and collaboration, Australia's healthcare system can better meet the needs of diverse communities. The future of hospitals is not just about buildings and beds, it is about creating flexible, responsive healthcare services that put people at the centre of care.

33

Privatising Care[27]

Public goods are concerned with basic human needs and services which are essential for participation in society, typically health, welfare, education, housing and transport. They exist where there are not natural markets or where markets cannot be reasonably expected to provide them in an equitable way, though they are frequently provided in conjunction with private sector markets. The recent history of public administration is of attempts to use market signals to manage the provision of public goods, harnessing the capacity of competition to drive efficiency.

Strategies have included the creation of internal markets (activity based funding in Acute hospitals), contracting with or otherwise utilising private sector markets (COAG public housing reforms) and outsourcing or privatising functions (disability employment services).

Difficulties in achieving desired outcomes are in part attributable to the failure to recognise some essential differences between public and private goods. Public goods are evaluated on three inter-related but competing dimensions: ***Efficiency***: the costs and benefits of the goods; ***Quality***: the relative value of the goods against qualitative criteria; and ***Access***: the availability on an equitable basis to those who have a claim on the goods.

In the private sector efficiency is dominant. The principal requirement is the creation of value for shareholders. Quality is derivative, failures of quality impact upon profitability through loss of market share or the creation of liability. Access is an outcome

---

27. Published in The Mandarin, 2020.

of the market; goods are provided when and where and to whom they can be profitably provided.

Utilising market based systems to provide public goods has had mixed success and frequent systemic failure. Activity Based Funding was very successful initially in driving efficiency in hospitals, but did so at the cost of quality as catering and cleaning services were slashed, nursing care was reduced, and emergency beds were forgone in order to optimise occupancy. Access was determined by efficiency and service availability was not based on population health planning. The COAG housing reforms in the late 90s transferred resources from the construction of social housing to the payment of rental subsidies to private landlords. The effect was to push up the cost of private rental by an equivalent amount, reducing the availability of affordable housing. The privatisation of disability employment services has resulted in an efficient system that meets targets for job placement but fails to meet the long term employment support needs of disabled people.

The situation in Victoria with respect to privatising services is complex and changing.

The provision of traditional welfare services has a long history of non-government participation. Following the 1850s gold rush many church and benevolent organisations were established with substantial resources committed to charitable works. During the 1970s and 80s as these resources became depleted and wages became a greater component of overall costs, many established child and family welfare organisations negotiated 100% subsidies of their costs. Subsequently these agreements were rolled into a unit price which is the subject of a "service contract", an agreement about price and volume. Quality provisions are not enforced. They do however address equity in that they reflect agreements that types and quantities of services are provided to eligible consumers in designated areas.

Most of the state's disability services are provided directly by the Department of Human Services though the NDIS will change that. Because of a strong public sector Union over a long period, wages and conditions have been relatively generous. An attempt in the early 90s to privatise the services failed because transmission of business requirements in industrial agreements would transfer these benefits to the non-government sector, increasing overall costs rather than reducing them.

Privatisation continues to be an issue in Victorian residential aged care. The State is unusual in that it owns and operates a large number of the residential aged care beds, largely attached to rural hospitals. State owned residential aged care services are subject to nurse/patient ratios and so are very much more expensive to operate than private sector beds, where personal care attendants are employed rather than nurses. Attempts by both the Kennett and Napthine governments to privatise the metropolitan residential aged care beds failed when they lost elections. The privatisation of nursing home beds preferences efficiency over quality and equity. It reduces costs by reducing the skill level of the workforce and beds can be relocated with their Commonwealth subsidies to profitable locations irrespective of need.

Aged care is marginally profitable and highly regulated. Recent policy changes have removed the distinction between low and high care beds and made the charging of accommodation bonds possible for all beds. Demand is reducing as consumers prefer care in their own homes and is increasingly for dementia care and end-of-life care. In order to survive, residential aged care providers run at close to total occupancy and have a high level of acuity (which determines the Commonwealth subsidy). The Abbott government was sympathetic to arguments from some large publicly listed companies for an uncapping of bed numbers and the provision of vouchers to consumers. This would remove the regulation of the industry and reduce the viability of small local services and equity of access.

The most significant move towards privatising of human services is an unintended consequence of patient centred purchasing of services. This was pioneered in Victoria in the disability sector, and it now underpins the NDIS and community aged care. It will become the dominant means of purchasing and providing services across the human services sector in coming years.

On the surface Consumer Directed Care looks like enhancing quality through increased accountability to consumers. Consumers are allocated a package of resources based on their assessed need, which they can use to flexibly "purchase" the services they require. In practice the purchasing is mediated through an authorised agency and packages are competed for in a market. In the last two funding rounds, allocations were mainly to corporate providers and nationally based not-for-profits to the exclusion of local providers. These organisations can "cream off" the lucrative case management components of packages and sub-contracted to local providers to provide services. The effect is de-facto privatisation.

There is a range of market based mechanisms which can and have been used to enhance the management of health and human services. If these are to deliver improved outcomes however, they need to attend to and balance the requirements of efficiency, quality and access which are fundamental requirement for the distribution of public goods.

34

Educational Rigidity or Learning?[28]

One of the advantages of being married to a teacher is that you experience at second hand, the way education is delivered.

I have had the value of some particular insights in the past year. A number of months ago my wife was documenting some work she had been doing with her Preps. She introduced them to felting and as part of the language and literacy aspect of the play program she asked them questions about their experience of the wool and what the experience meant to them. She then recorded verbatim their individual comments.

I would have to say that the comments these 5 and 6 year olds made were astounding. They showed a remarkably subtle and individual grasp of language and a very advanced implicit understanding of metaphor. On another occasion, these same children were asked to talk about eyes and seeing. Again, their responses were astounding. This was for Dylan Thomas "the colour of saying"; to be as he described himself as a young boy "in love with the shape and sound of words"

And I thought, this is where literacy begins; not with recognising words on paper but in the discovery of the rich texture of language and the articulation of one's own voice.

I was curious so I asked how these children were going against the objective measures of literacy. I found that the indicator of achievement had been increased that year from level 5 to level 10 for reading. Two thirds of the way through the year, 2 children

---
28. Published *Border Mail*, 2017.

were slightly below the indicator. The majority were in the 15 range and a small number were reading at level 25. There was, as you would expect, a bell curve, but one which was massively skewed towards achievement.

What struck me was that here we had a program inspired by the Reggio Emilia educational philosophy that was relationship based; child centred, not caught up with enforced conformity of iPad programs and other screen based activities, and focused on the complete cognitive, social and emotional development of the children. There is no do doubt why parents loved it so much. In the thirty years that I have been involved with education, this was the most inspiring and successful early childhood education program that I have seen.

Of course, that program has now been largely closed down. Most of the experienced teachers who established it have been moved out. Their inventive initiatives which build upon play have been replaced by traditional literacy programs of the sort that had been abandoned years ago because they don't work. The current obsession of education officialdom with testing and data collection about performance has muscled out engagement with children as individual learners.

We pay a price for imposing rigidity in learning on young children; a price that we can see in the increasing numbers of children in our primary schools who cannot settle or attend to tasks; have diminished sensory development and are socially and emotionally fragile. As noted, paediatric occupational therapist Angela Hanscom wrote in a recent article in the Washington Post: "If children are not given enough natural movement and play experiences, they start their academic careers with a disadvantage. They are more likely to be clumsy, have difficulty paying attention, trouble controlling their emotions, utilise poor problem-solving methods, and demonstrate difficulties with social interactions."

A recent research summary on Play and Learning by Dr Rachel White, from the Institute of Child Development, University of Minnesota noted that the scientific research supports that child-centred play is learning; including social, object, pretend, physical, and media play. "Through play, children learn to regulate their behaviour, lay the foundations for later learning in science and mathematics, figure out the complex negotiations of social relationships, build a repertoire of creative problem solving skills, and so much more."

A contrast to our assessment obsessed, increasingly rigid education system can be seen in Finland. Finland has consistently performed among the top nations on the Program for International Student Assessment (PISA), a standardised test given to 15-year olds in 65 nations and territories around the world. Finnish children start compulsory, early childhood education at age 7. They spend a sizable part of each day playing, not filling out worksheets. Finnish students do not take a national, standardised high-stakes test until they matriculate secondary school and then only if they intend to enter higher education. The purpose of assessment in Finland is to improve learning.

We all want the best for our children. For some, this means strictly "benchmarking" achievements in the earliest years, in the hope that this will magically improve an ATAR score in year 12. Most parents, however, want their children to start their education experience in a safe supportive environment which encourages them to love learning and enhances their individual development.

Early childhood education needs to focus on the whole child and meet them at their level of development rather than requiring that they conform with confected standards.

35

Politics and the State of Health[29]

Health policy impacts almost every aspect of our lives and so it is surprising that the major parties are giving little attention to Health in this election.

Rural Australia has relatively poor health.

The electorates of Farrer and Indi have high rates of chronic disease and far too many preventable deaths. They have high rates of profound and severe disability. The region is ageing and requires a greatly increased level of home based care.

Too many children are failing to meet developmental milestones.

There are shortages of doctors, nurses and allied health professionals and a potential crisis in the availability of obstetrics, general surgery and emergency medicine.

We need to promote healthier lifestyles, provide access to early intervention through GPs and other primary health care professionals and integrated treatment programs for chronic conditions.

A comprehensive regional mental health strategy is required to provide for the seriously mentally ill, including step-down care for those discharged from acute services.

Primary mental health services are required for depression and anxiety and early intervention, child and adolescent psychiatric services and early psychosis services for children and young people.

Capital for rural and regional health services needs to be continued and expanded.

---

29. Published in the Border Mail, March 2013.

Albury Wodonga Health needs the resources and infrastructure to serve a regional population of 150,000 people.

Ageing in place requires home care packages to meet community need. Residential aged care must be affordable and of high quality.

So, how do the major parties and candidates stack up against these challenges?

Labor in government achieved much. Benchmark funding for health was restored, Local Hospital Networks established, and Activity Based Funding for hospitals initiated. There were preventative health and national workforce strategies. Medical student numbers were effectively doubled. Medicare Locals were established to coordinate primary care. Capital funds were provided from which Albury Wodonga's Regional Cancer Centre was funded.

Labor's policy proposes continuing health reform with a stronger emphasis upon primary health care. Labor has not however indicated initiatives which will address the particular needs of Indi and Farrer.

The Coalition Health Policy is light-on. Proposed stronger local governance and activity based funding are already happening. The Private Health Insurance subsidy is failed policy. Workforce initiatives are limited, and preventative health does not get a mention. Only in the areas of Mental Health and coordinated care for diabetes does policy address the important health challenges.

The Coalition has not addressed local issues. Mr Dutton supports additional activity funding for Albury Wodonga Health but has committed no funds. Ms Mirabella failed in office and in opposition to make a contribution to Health.

The Greens propose publicly funded dental care, improved access through local community health centres and a national approach to injury prevention and rehabilitation. They would restrict junk food advertising and improve food labelling.

Of the remaining candidates in Indi, Cathy McGowan provides a health policy most in line with local health needs. She proposes a national approach to workforce development and local planning for mental health. She has policy on aged care availability and funding and. supports the need for capital infrastructure.

In an election in which Health is largely being ignored, the candidate giving most thought to local health needs is Cathy McGowan.

Section 4: *In Majorca Alfonso watched the door*

> Yet God (that hews mountain and continent,
> Earth, all, out; who, with trickling increment,
> Veins violets and tall trees makes more and more)
> Could crowd career with conquest while there went
> Those years and years by of world without event
> That in Majorca Alfonso watched the door.
> *Gerard Manly Hopkins: from In Honour of*
> *St. Alphonsus Rodriguez*

36

McAbbott: A Scottish Tale[30]

A tragedy of thwarted ambition in Canberra.

The Cast:

MacAbbott: Thane of Glamis, and Thane of Cawdor and North Sydney whose overweening ambition causes him to murder the previous ruler using subterfuge and lies. Once he is King, he is found to have risen many times above his level of incompetence and is vulnerable to revolt. Rightly describes his reign as "a tale told by an idiot: full of sound and fury, signifying nothing".

Lady Credlin MacAbbott: The power behind the throne, urging McAbbott on to deeds of greater brutality and incompetence. Mostly seen sharpening spears and dismissing miscreants from the Court ("Out, out damned spot")

Duncan Rudd McGillard: A talented but flawed leadership that was brought to an end in a bloody slaughter. Made vulnerable by irreconcilable internal contradictions.

Joe Banquo: Fellow traveller of McAbbott before being slain. Witness to the prophesied end but unable to comprehend its significance. Despite his demise, he is seen to haunt the party in the later Acts in the form of a budget that will not die.

---
30. For John Rimmer. Who enjoyed this at the time it was written.

Fleance McCorbann: Son of Banquo. He escapes the murderers sent to kill him and his father and takes a princeling job with the OECD.

Malcolm: Considered by some to be the true successor to King Duncan Rudd McGillard. Claimed to be "none of woman born", but those on the right of the court have an alternative reflection on the legitimacy of his parentage. He returns to claim the throne in a bloody revolt. A sequel dealing with his rule may be a tragedy, a comedy or a farce.

Lady Bronnie McDuff: An insubstantial figure, prone to extravagance and hovering about ("Whither should I fly"). Her execution sets in train the missteps which will eventually bring McAbbott down.

Morrison McDuff: Banished to Human Services, he attempts to live down his reputation for brutality but just can't help himself. He has overweening ambition ("If it be mine, Keep it not from me, quickly let me have it.") and is the hope of the Right. He returns to the centre of the action in the hope of delivering Mc Abbott a fatal blow.

The Weird Sisters (Murdoch, Jones and Bolt): The three witches who tell MacAbbott the prophesy that he will be king and set the wheels into motion that eventually destroy him. Urgers from the wings, they form an amorphous composite character which is liable to disappear into hot air. Critical opinion is divided as whether they are the personification of evil or just a gaggle of old women.

37

"Just don't call us saints!"[31]

I met Siobhan on a windswept morning in Rosslare, County Wexford on the south eastern tip of Ireland. I was conducting focus groups in the early stages of setting up the first national survey of carers of the intellectually disabled in Ireland. I was interested in hearing first hand about the experiences of those who had chosen to keep family members in their care rather than place them in the largely institutional care facilities in Ireland.

Siobhan was in her late sixties. She had driven that morning form Tramore, an hour and a half away on winding Irish roads, in some of the foulest weather I have come across. As we waited for others to arrive she explained that she had cared for her son as a single parent for over forty years. For much of this time there had not been pensions and few services. The choice was to place your family member in care or receive nothing.

When two other women arrived, whose stories were very similar, Siobhan winked at them and said to their combined laughter "Now, just don't call us saints". She explained that their experience was very consistent. Each new person representing government or service providers had, within minutes then left without providing any assistance.

She explained that they had had forty years of platitudes. Everyone was so supportive and so admiring of the care they

---
[31]. Published Border Mail October 2008. This article was published prior to the establishment of the NDIS.

provided. But what they were not prepared to do was to take them seriously, and to provide real assistance which would make a difference to their lives.

In my experience of working with disabled people and their families in Australia, the picture here is not very different. It is true that our services are more extensive and a lot of work has gone into planning for services which will make it possible for people with disabilities to lead happy and fulfilled lives in the community. But the care system rides on the back of families who are often stretched to breaking point. Services are still far too inflexible and families are frequently forced to fit in with what is on offer rather what their family member needs at this point in time.

A report was released earlier this year which gave some indication of the financial costs experienced by families with a disabled member. The costs are great and for the most part they fall upon women who sacrifice careers and provide untold and unacknowledged hours of care. The lump sum addition to the carers benefit announced by the government at the end of last year was welcome but was a pittance compared to the actual financial and emotional costs involved.

About 2.5 million Australians aged 15 years and over care for someone at home because of a disability or old age. Women are more likely than men to be carers. Of parents aged between 35 and 54 years, 22 per cent of mothers and 15 per cent of fathers are carers. And about half of these parent carers are caring for a child with a disability. Almost half of all parents caring for a child with a disability say they need more access to respite care.

The message that I heard from Siobhan and those other women in Rosslare, was the same as I had heard over and over again from parent support groups in Victoria. Supportive words are not a substitute for supportive actions. Disabled people have very individual needs. They need services which respond to their very specific needs, and they have to get those services when they need them, not at some ill-defined point in the future.

And most of all, the plea from carers is to be taken seriously. They know their family member better than anyone else. No-one has a more genuine and sustained interest in their wellbeing. Yes they can be over-protective and yes they can be blind to the needs of others who also need assistance, but would any of us be less of an advocate for a family member of our own who needed assistance? And in my experience, their requests are modest.

We all owe a great deal to people like Siobhan and the many hundreds of carers in our own community. They deserve our help and acknowledgement. Just don't call them saints!

38

Abuse in Ireland's Industrial Schools[32]

In 1946, Fr. Edward Flanagan, the founder of Boy's Town in Nebraska, returned to his native Ireland. He was feted there as befitted a man who had committed his life to the care of others, and whose achievements had been portrayed by Hollywood in an academy award winning film. However, his message, which highlighted the abusive and destructive practices in Ireland's industrial schools, was unwelcome. In a pattern which is all too familiar church leaders and politicians excoriated him as ill-informed and mischievous. Fr Flanagan's brief campaign, well informed as it was by local sources, did not survive his sudden death in 1948.

Mary Raftery and Eoin O'Sullivan's book, Suffer the Little Children, delves deeply into the dark history of Ireland's industrial schools. Though they were often called orphanages, many of the children placed in industrial schools were not orphans. Nor were they primarily children of unmarried mothers who were a small percentage of those detained. These institutions were defined by their role as industrial training schools.

Ireland's industrial schools had their origins in late nineteenth century legislation to provide for children deemed to be in need of care and control outside the workhouses established under the 1838 Poor Law. These schools expanded in the late 19th and early 20th centuries due to widespread poverty and concerns about Protestant proselytizing among poor children.

---

32. This review Appeared in Tain, December 2001.

Throughout the latter half of the 20th century, fifty-two industrial schools in Ireland housed over 150,000 children. At their peak they "cared" for 8,000 children. Principally Catholic religious orders operated them, although local parishes managed two. The largest providers were the Christian Brothers and the Sisters of Mercy. Others included the Oblate Fathers, the Rosminians, and the Daughters of Charity. Many industrial schools were co-located with schools for the middle classes, and in some cases, the infamous Magdalen laundries, where "immoral" women were detained.

It was not until 1970 that the Kennedy Committee, established by the minister for education, against the advice of his department, to inquire into the industrial school system, exposed an appallingly mismanaged and inadequate system of care for Ireland's dispossessed young. Though the Kennedy Committee report was to herald the end of Ireland's squalid Industrial School system, it was another three years before it saw the light of day and more than another decade before many of its recommendations were implemented. The twenty years since have seen a continuing expose of scandals associated with these facilities. This culminated in 1999 with the award-winning documentary States of Fear, which presented the horrific stories of survivors from their own perspective.

Suffer the Little Children was written by Mary Raftery, producer of States of Fear, and Dr Eoin O'Sullivan, social policy analyst and lecturer at Trinity College, Dublin. It catalogues powerfully a history of sustained abuse: horrific beatings, starvation, forced labour and commercial exploitation, sexual assault, deprivation of education, humiliation, and denial of affection.

Recalling his time at St Joseph's Industrial School in Kilkenny, former resident Ed stated, "I cried when they brought me back to St Joseph's, to all that pain and abuse and torment. I wanted to stay in prison, but they wouldn't let me. I have no happy memories of my childhood. I don't remember a single good day."

Raftery and O'Sullivan dismiss the now familiar arguments used to mitigate the responsibility for this abuse by the religious orders: that the abuse was the actions of "a few rotten apples', that the term 'sexual abuse' had not been defined at the time and as a concept was not well understood; that the institutions were under-funded by the State; and that the methods of care, particularly with respect to corporal punishment, were consistent with prevailing social norms.

The authors demonstrate that the abuse was not incidental or episodic, but ubiquitous and endemic. They show that while more is now known about child sexual abuse, its prevalence was well understood by government, Gardai and religious leaders. They show that while the funding for child care was never lavish, it was consistently higher, on a per capita basis, than the weekly income of the families from which the children were taken. Survivors consistently report that they were better fed and received better care in their own families. They demonstrate that the excessive physical punishment meted out upon defenceless children was proscribed from the earliest stages by the founders of the religious congregations that practised them and was consistently outside the guidelines of the responsible government department.

While it recounts the experiences of many survivors, the focus remains on the systemic failures that enabled widespread abuse, rather than solely on the individual perpetrators. Its conclusions about that system are compelling. The industrial schools were in essence a commercial operation. Britain, with similar beginnings and the same legislative base, abandoned the discredited congregate care model of care for children fifty years earlier than Ireland where the church hierarchy actively discouraged fostering. Despite claims that care was provided for these children by the charity of the religious, it was paid in fact for by the Irish State. The farm produce of the institutions, which was generated by forced labour and never accounted for, augmented capitation rates paid by the State.

The system enforced the moral authoritarianism of the church and functioned in such a way as to reinforce the rigid class distinctions of the country. Its subjects were the poor. The children of the schools were kept apart from the children of the middle classes except where they were required to be their servants. In a cruel irony, while many were placed in the schools for truancy, they received little in the way of education and, on leaving, were placed as unskilled farm workers or domestic servants.

The system survived because of the complicity of the State. This was in part neglect; a failure to inspect, monitor and enforce guidelines. Its deeper origins however are in the conception of the Irish State. The State conceived itself as minimalist. The task of caring for the vulnerable was understood as the responsibility of the church and the family. It is only in the past decade that the Irish State has come to accept that its children may be failed by both their families and the church, and the State may have to take active responsibility for their care.

This book is a work of scholarship written for the general reader. It will find an audience amongst those with an historical interest and those interested in the relationship between church and State. It has also some important lessons for those outside Ireland working in out-of-home care and those managing or regulating it.

Wherever there is vulnerability there will be those willing to exploit it, whether for profit, for personal gratification or out of sheer malice. This is true of the care of the young, the disabled and of the elderly. One abiding rationale for the State is the protection of the vulnerable. Vigilance by the State is not sufficient, however, to ensure safety in care. It must be expressed in processes which establish standards, and which systematically monitor performance against them.

Abusive practice proliferates in closed systems. Raftery and O'Sullivan quote Irish playwright Patricia Burke Brogan, herself formerly a Mercy Sisters novice, who left the congregation in protest at the treatment of women in the order's laundries: "Total unquestioning obedience like that is a very dangerous concept. If you close your mind and you don't allow questions to be asked, the danger is very great that abuse of that power can happen."

The best defence against disturbed practices is transparency. The resistance by the managers of Ireland's industrial schools to proposed external visitors is instructive.

When care is given over to the ignorant, the untrained or the basely motivated, its subjects are at risk. There is a lesson here for the would-be privatisers of contemporary services. Good care requires sustained attention over time by a committed and well-trained workforce. It cannot be purchased as dehumanised service units.

It is fashionable these days to decry deinstitutionalisation as the cynical cost cutting. Services, which are poorly resourced and managed, are a poor alternative. We should not, however, lose sight of the fact that the old institutions for the care of children, the intellectually disabled and the mentally ill were evil places. Not because the people who worked there and managed them were evil, (though Raftery and O'Sullivan give many examples of where this was the case) but because of the imbalance of power that was their hallmark. At their core, these institutions were built on the power imbalance between carers and those in their care, often with devastating consequences.

39

The Host of the Air[33]

Chancellor, Vice-Chancellor, Graduands, Members of the University, distinguished guests.

I would like if I may, to share with you, some lines from the poet William Butler Yeats. The poem is The Host of the Air:

> O'Driscoll drove with a song,
> The wild duck and the drake,
> From the tall and the tufted weeds
> Of the drear Hart Lake.
>
> And he saw how the weeds grew dark
> At the coming of night tide,
> And he dreamed of the long dim hair
> Of Bridget his bride.
>
> He heard while he sang and dreamed
> A piper piping away,
> And never was piping so sad,
> And never was piping so gay.

Yeats was dealing, in a very evocative way, with one of the great periods of social change, the coming of Christianity to Northern Europe. It was a time of change about which he was profoundly ambivalent. He was excited by the energy and the dynamic of

---

33. Graduation Address, La Trobe University, 1998.

change, but he saw also its destructive power, the casting away of the old druidic traditions. "The bread and the wine were a doom", he says "for these were the host of the air".

> And never was piping so sad,
> And never was piping so gay.

Delivering the Graduation Address, La Trobe University

It is in this ambivalence that I believe that Yeats has something to say to us.

You see, we are ourselves living through a time of momentous change, change that will bring with it great opportunities for most of us here today. As we move from a manufacturing based economy to a knowledge based one, as we increasingly operate on a global basis, there will be fewer boundaries to our potential. As a society, our capacity to produce and to communicate has been immeasurably increased over the past twenty years. But our progress is not without cost. While these changes will bring great opportunities, this will not be true for everyone. For many, change is a source of opportunity and fortune, but the costs and benefits of social change fall unevenly, and for some, these changes will be source of great misfortune.

Today is a day of great rejoicing and I do not wish to dampen it. I do, however want to give some examples of the way some of the costs and benefits of change are apportioned.

We have as a consequence of technological and structural change in the economy, the greatest disparity in wealth in this country at any time since the depression. The difference between the top ten percent by income and the bottom ten percent is substantial and growing. As we move from a manufacturing economy to a knowledge based economy, we are fundamentally refashioning the means of production, distribution and exchange. In the process we are largely eliminating unskilled and semi-skilled labour from the workforce. The winners are those who are young, mobile, unencumbered by the obligations to care or to provide for others, those who are highly skilled and educated in knowledge based industries.

The losers are those largely middle aged men in traditional forms of employment, with limited skills and with family responsibilities.

This has a rural subtext, because in rural areas, people are often locationally encumbered also. What do you do if you are a 50 year old, unemployed, Wodonga meat worker. Another subtext is that of the single parents who continue to be amongst the most economically disadvantaged because of the responsibility to care, and who nowadays face diminishing support. For those who are employed in traditional areas, their relative position is declining because in these industries, workplace reform is almost invariably a euphemism for real wage reduction.

My second area of concern is with the costs to small rural communities. Small towns have been declining for more than 30 years. This has been a function of:

- The impact post war of mechanisation and the reduced requirement for labour.
- A greater variety of employment options for young people located in cities.
- An ageing population overall; and
- Globalisation of commodity markets, such that efficiency in production is paramount.

Agricultural economists have a rule of thumb. If you want to remain viable you must double your land holding every generation. This means that you must acquire your neighbour's property or sell yours and the farming community is halved on average every 30 to 40 years.

There are some specific things happening now however, which are rapidly increasing the rate of decline of rural communities.

Firstly, the information revolution is reducing the locationally determined transactional activity of employers. We see this most dramatically with banks that are progressively closing rural outlets. But other businesses are also able to rationalise payroll and accounts payable functions. They are left then only with a customer services function which is increasingly operated through a Post Office or bureau.

Secondly, the growth in the gaming industry is having a powerfully destructive impact upon small communities. There is strong anecdotal evidence of decline in retail activity as disposable income moves away from local retail outlets and into large centres. Smaller communities lose activity but do not get the gains associated with increased employment associated with gaming. This is one of the most dramatic instances of which I am aware, of redistribution of resources away from individuals and communities and towards corporate interests.

Thirdly, the privatisation of utilities will see further reductions of employment in rural work crews and in regional centres Private firms do not have or accept community obligations in the way public ones do. This can be seen also in the privatising and rationalising of local government services.

There is loss of essential infrastructure. As Regional Director of Health. I fought to maintain small rural hospitals, if not as acute hospitals, then as dispensers of more broadly defined health services, because of their centrality for small communities. I believe that it will become progressively harder to do this.

Nowadays 70% of farms are reliant upon off-farm income to remain viable. That means that part time work in hospitals and schools is critical for the survival of farming communities. If you lose the infrastructure, you lose the community.

But there are more general social costs. Do we believe that with the decline of the family farm for instance, it is acceptable to have two paddocks between here and Yarrawonga, or for that land to be farmed principally by foreign owned feed lots. The family farm will put in a crop every year because this is its livelihood. An absentee will do so when it is profitable. Do we want our local food supply and our export income to be so dependent.

And there are social costs for individuals. A growing section of the community finds itself left behind while the rest of us move on.

> And never was piping so sad,
> And never was piping so gay.

Finally, there are costs associated with social change for many men. Much of men's sense of themselves is tied to their experience of work. But many of the traditional models of men's work are changing.

- We have a steady but inexorable disappearance of most unskilled and semi-skilled labour, usually in traditional "male" areas of work.
- We are seeing much higher participation rates by women. The majority of new jobs are part-time and in service industries, traditionally work dominated by women.
- There is increasing employment in knowledge based industries, often at home.
- While there is continuing exclusion of women from managerial positions (because of inflexible work times) there is increasing dominance of women in the professions.

Once past 45 years of age, if a male becomes unemployed, it is unlikely that he will work again in conventional employment.

While traditional work patterns have changed, the relationship context for men has changed also.

- Increasingly their partners are employed, they have their own circle of friends and are affirmed outside the home.
- Their partners have multiple roles, mother, professional, workmate etc.

- They may well contribute more financially to the home than their male partner
- Traditional patterns of dominance in relationships have (rightly) gone.

Henry David Thoreau said, "The mass of men lead lives of quiet desperation". While he was speaking generically, he could in our time be speaking in a gender specific way. I think that many men are finding it desperately hard to come to terms with the changes in their economic and social environment. This is the more so in rural areas where relationships, roles and expectations are generally traditional.

None of us would want to turn back the clock The past was not a golden age. It was particularly not a golden age if you were black, disabled or even if you were a woman. We cannot afford to be fearful of the future. Change will come whether we like it or not. Some of the more ignorant and uninformed comments made in recent times about immigration and indigenous affairs seem to me to be born principally from a fear of the future and of the uncertainty that change brings. But if the past should not be idealised then perhaps the future is also not without alloy.

I have spoken from the perspective of social policy but there are issues of ambivalence towards change for universities also. There has been much discussion in recent times about the function of the university in modern society. There are some who would argue that universities should look backwards, should concern themselves with traditional areas of scholarship only, and not engage with a contemporary world. In particular, they should not seek to prepare people for careers in the new and emerging professions.

But surely the university must concern itself with the new and in fact, be the source of new knowledge. It must be at the cutting edge of change as we seek to come to terms with this new world and with the challenges it will place before us.

At the same time, the university has traditionally been and must continue to be, the guardian of our knowledge, our wisdom and our culture.

We should not be persuaded that that these roles are mutually exclusive. The propositions that a university should be either not contemporary or not value the past, are equally unacceptable.

You are graduating to day with everything before. You are young or making a new start. You are intelligent and hardworking, or you would not be here today. You are well trained by fine teachers, and you have a degree from one of the county's most distinguished institutions. Who could stand against you?

What is more, you commence your careers at a critical time of change and opportunity. And you must absolutely grasp your opportunities with both hands. You must fashion the new world.

In Yeats's terms you must be attentive to the powerful music of change and be excited by its potential. I urge you also however, to be alive to the nuances in that music; to hear the sad notes also, and to remember as you grasp that future which you so richly deserve, that the cost of your success is at least in part being borne by others.

> And never was piping so sad,
> And never was piping so gay.

I congratulate you and wish you well.

With Gough Whitlam at La Trobe University Albury Wodonga graduation

40

Willian Smith O'Brien – An Irishman in Australia[34]

William Smith O'Brien is an important link between mid-nineteenth century Ireland and Australia. O'Brien was a much maligned and underestimated figure in republican history, whose contribution has in recent years been re-evaluated and acknowledged by the Republic. A new book by Robert Sloan which deals principally with his career as a parliamentarian and rebel rather than his time as a political prisoner in Van Diemens Land will make an important contribution to that re-evaluation.

The statue of Smith O'Brien that stands in O'Connell St Dublin, is relatively small, and is located between the more imposing monuments to the giants of nineteenth century Irish nationalism, Daniel O'Connell and Charles Stuart Parnell. The size and location are appropriate. O'Brien, and the Young Ireland Movement with which he became associated late in his political career, occupy an important place in the evolution of Irish nationalism from the political activism epitomised by O'Connell to its fusing with social activism in the alliance between Parnell and the Land League later in the nineteenth century.

O'Brien was of the Protestant Upper Middle Class ascendancy which produced so many of the nation's nationalist leaders of the nineteenth century. He was an O'Brien of Thomond (Clare) and Dromoland, a direct descendant of Brian Boru, and as such counted amongst his ancestors Kings of Munster and of all Ireland. He took

---

34. Published in *Tain*.

this legacy very seriously, seeing in it an obligation to serve his country fearlessly. After an undistinguished University career, he found himself a Member of Parliament under the system of rotating preference of the landed gentry, which still operated in the 1830s. As suffrage was extended, he was consistently returned by popular (if restricted) vote, including in 1847 when he was effectively drafted by the constituency.

His seventeen year parliamentary record is impressive. He remained apart from the O'Connellites and pursued a personal if increasingly nationalistic agenda. He opposed coercion through the Arms Bill of 1843 and again in 1846. He championed the reform of tithes and supported the introduction of a Poor Law for Ireland which reflected that of Britain. He argued passionately for education and incurred the wrath of the clergy for opposing sectarian education, which he saw as dividing the nation and breeding intolerance. With Thomas Wyse, in 1843, he came close to uniting the disparate group of Protestant Liberals in opposition to Peel's repressive laws. His disruptive tactics in the house brought it to a standstill, foreshadowing those which Parnell was to perfect forty years later.

Amongst the list of failed nationalist endeavours which have been frequent in Irish history, the Young Ireland rebellion of 1848 has been rated as the least. This despite the fact that its leaders were amongst the most intelligent and its impetus one of the greatest human tragedies to befall the nation.

The rising which O'Brien lead in 1848 was precipitated by the revolutions which took place that year in Europe, both in the revolutionary enthusiasm that they encouraged amongst the disaffected, and the anxiety that they generated within the ascendancy. As coercion became more severe, revolutionary fervour increased. But for all the talk of revolt, the rebellion was ill-prepared and doomed to failure.

The leader of Young Ireland's only rebellion could never entirely reconcile himself to revolution and insisted that the rag-tag army that he led through South Tipperary, damage no property and pay for everything it consumed. Betrayed by local clergy and largely deserted by his army, O'Brien's rebellion collapsed into farce at the widow McCormack cottage in Ballingarry.

The British authorities of the day were more astute than their successors in 1916 in putting down rebellion and managing its aftermath. They had exploited the divisions between the O'Connellites and Young Ireland over the legitimacy of violent rebellion and of co-operation with the Whigs in Westminster. This dispute was aggravated by O'Connell's death and could perhaps have been resolved by no one other than O'Brien who commanded the respect of both factions. The transportation of Mitchell and the imprisonment of Duffy awaiting trial, removed the intellectual leadership of the movement at a critical time but also re-enforced the urgency of revolt. When the skirmish at Ballingarry occurred, its incompetence and futility were mercilessly exploited. Most importantly, the British resisted the temptation to execute the leaders and transported them instead. They thus ensured that O'Brien and his associates were viewed as fools rather than martyrs. Robert Emmett's rising of 1802 was every bit as ill-advised and lacking in competence as O'Brien's in 1848. Emmett however wears a martyr's crown.

The rebellion of 1848 failed for many reasons, not least of which was O'Brien's incompetence as a commander. He had no training or aptitude for military leadership. He sought to avoid the role but having accepted it, believed he was honour bound to pursue it to its end. Christopher Koch's projection of him as the effete and inconsequential Fitzgibbon in his recent novel Out of Ireland does him an injustice.

Ironically perhaps O'Brien's greatest contribution to revolutionary politics was his recruitment to the rebellion, of a young James Stephens. Stephens, an early Fenian, who in 1858 formed the Irish Republican Brotherhood with Thomas Clarke Luby, John O'Mahony and Jeremiah O'Donovan Rossa, served as his *aide-de-camp*, and revered O'Brien's memory all his days.

O'Brien was in the end a man of contradictions. A social conservative, his political position moved over time from that of unionist to federalist, to repealer, and finally to republican as his understanding of his country's suffering and of the cynicism of Westminster grew. An, at times reluctant parliamentarian, he provided one of the few examples of effective constitutional politics in Ireland's interests between the hey-days of O'Connell and of Parnell. A reluctant leader, he came to be seen as the only public figure who could bring together the factions of mid nineteenth century Irish politics. A fiercely independent man whose career almost faltered on a number of occasions because he would not subserve his conscience or his judgement to the political power of O'Connell or of popular sentiment, he came to lead a peasant army whose cause he championed, but whose methods he opposed.

Throughout however, he emerges as a man of integrity, whose life became devoted to the wellbeing of his countryman. As a parliamentarian his achievements were significant and but for the farce of Ballingarry, they would be celebrated alongside those of Flood, Grattan, O'Connell, Butt and Parnell. If he lacked the political opportunism of O'Connell, the revolutionary ardour of Meagher and the intellectual brilliance of Davis, Duffy and Mitchell, his moral strength was respected by his most sever critics.

O'Brien was, however, also a man out of his time. The political environment was fundamentally changed by the famine. If the French revolution was to ensure that political rights would dominate the revolutionary agenda for the first fifty years of the century, the terrible suffering of the Irish people during the 1840's created an environment whereby social and economic rights would dominate the second half century. The subsequent years would be dominated by the struggle for land and tenancy reform. It took Parnell's astuteness to forge the linkage between parliamentary leadership and social and economic reform. O'Brien was amongst the few in Westminster to argue with passion for changed policy to alleviate Ireland's suffering during the famine. He was, however, a prisoner of his class. He sought political reform and abhorred social revolution.

O'Brien had another life after Ballingarry; as a convict in Van Diemens Land, and as respected speaker and elder statesman on his return to Europe in 1854. He did not again assume public office however and preferred a life of relative obscurity. Sloan's book does not address these later stages of his life.

Sloan's biography makes an important contribution to scholarship concerning mid nineteenth century Irish nationalism. It is a lucid account of the political development of an undervalued and frequently misunderstood figure in the politics of the time. It is well argued and referenced meticulously. It is particularly strong in elucidating the political factionalism at Westminster during the time. It is less strong however in establishing the social context within which the formal politics of the time took place. Sloan documents well O'Brien's parliamentary activities in response to the famine, but the famine's broader social significance and its significance in framing the political environment for the remainder of the century are largely unexamined.

William Smith O'Brien is deserving of his statue in O'Connell Street, and the belated attempt by the Irish Republic to recognise his contribution. Robert Sloan's well-written biography will make that recognition the easier.

41

Travelling North[35]

I went north to Belfast on Good Friday. It is an auspicious day for the north of Ireland. It was eleven years to the day that the accord that formalised the peace process was signed and "the troubles" officially ended. I had been to Belfast often before, but on those occasions I had not ventured past the leafy environs of Queens University in South Belfast, an area relatively untouched by the violence that had convulsed the community since the early seventies.

On this occasion I wanted to learn more. The peace, if not shattered, had been threatened by two incidents in a fortnight in which senseless murders had taken place by a group claiming continuity with the IRA. There was a strong sense that all it would take would be retaliation from the protestant paramilitaries to restart the violent enmity.

For all its suffering Belfast is a grand and increasingly vibrant city. I had been warned that its traditions of dour Presbyterianism would render Belfast a solemn town on Good Friday. I had been misled. Shops were open all day and you could get a drink if you waited until after 5.00pm, which was not the case on this day in Dublin. The central business area was alive and dozens of construction projects testified to Britain and the European Union's commitment to reinforcing the peace process by investment.

The power sharing arrangements at Storemont, the Northern Ireland Parliament, are now well established, but beneath the formal political changes there are also significant social changes.

---
35. Published in Border Mail, 2009.

The decline of unionist control over the economy and the exclusion of the nationalist community are symbolically represented now by the lone standing crane above the once mighty Harland and Wolff shipyard which lies dormant. Nationalists, excluded from industry for so many years, have found their way through education into the professions and in doing so have refashioned the community.

Below the surface however, old tensions persist. How could it be otherwise? There has been too much suffering, too much loss of life to easily forget the past. The memorial to the "Clonard martyrs" who died in 1969 when Bombay Street was firebombed by marauders from the Shankill, is a solemn reminder of what has gone before. The Unionist murals of the Shankill recall victories in seventeenth century battles and those of the Nationalist Falls Road laud martyrs of more recent struggles.

While the "peace wall" that separates the communities of the Falls and the Shankill is now an attraction for tourists who write their hopes for a sustainable peace on it, it continues to act as a barrier impeding transverse movement between the two communities. The gates are still locked down at night.

In Derry, a less prosperous town, the tensions are more obvious still. On Saturday nights rocks are still thrown from and into the Bogside. "Free Derry" corner stands intact and its murals record the horrors of Bloody Sunday 1972, when twenty seven unarmed civil rights marchers were shot by British paratroopers and thirteen died. The Saville Inquiry, established as part of the peace process to report on the events of that terrible day has yet to report and for many until it does, there can be no letting go of the past.

When the recent violent attacks took place, Martin McGuinness, reputedly once the hard man of the Derry IRA and now Second Minister in the power sharing government, stood beside his unionist counterpart and condemned those responsible as traitors. The word on the street was that though the words came hard, it was a sentiment shared in the Bogside and along the Falls.

There was consensus amongst those with whom I spoke. No-one with the exception of a small number of the implacable at the extremes of the two communities, wants to go back to the horrors of the past.. For nationalists, the issues that first brought them onto the streets; equal suffrage, adequate housing, access to welfare supports and employment, have been provided through the power sharing arrangements. For Unionists, the old hegemony has been surrendered but it is seen as a reasonable price to pay for peace.

While healing will take many more years, most believe that "the troubles" have passed.

With Gerry Adams, President of Sinn Fein, Allan Keating and Sam Keating in Melbourne, 2004

42

A tour around Dublin in poetry and song[36]

Elly, I am so pleased that you and Tim will have some time in Dublin on your trip and no doubt retrace many of our steps from when we were all there together in 2001.

I have jotted down some points of interest in Dublin which are marked for me by literature and song. You may encounter some of the places that have been of interest to me in that great city.

If you head from where you are staying in Sandymount, along Sandymount Rd towards Dublin Bay, you will pass the Star of the Sea Church. This is the place in which James Joyce sets the famous scene in Ulysses where Leopold Bloom encounters Gerty MacDowell. It is this section of the book, rather than Molly Bloom's soliloquy, which caused Ulysses to be banned in the US as obscene. By today's standards it will appear tame but at the time was seen as shocking. It is wonderful writing.

You can walk down Beach Road to Sandymount Strand, one of my favourite places in Dublin. Ireland and the world's great poet Seamus Heaney lived on Strand Road until his death last year. His wife Marie lives there still. She is a writer and scholar in her own right who translated the early Irish legends, including the Children of Lir and Finn McCool and the Salmon of Knowledge that I read to you as a child.

You can ask as you walk along the Strand, as Stephen Daedalus did, and I in his wake:

---

36. Written for my daughter Eloise for her visit with her husband Tim to Dublin.

"Am I walking into eternity along Sandymount strand?"

I used to walk here every morning while you and the others were still asleep. It extends down to connect with Rock Road and the bottom of Booterstown Road where we stayed. You can see from here the wide arc of Dublin Bay. In the words of Joyce's Finnegan's Wake:

> *"riverrun, past Eve and Adam's, from swerve of shore to bend of bay"*

Howth is to the north, a great place for a day trip on the DART. To the south you can see Dún Laoghaire where the ferries from Holyhead dock. The next outcrop is Sandy Cove where Joyce set the opening scenes of Ulysses. The Martello Tower and the Forty Foot Swimming hole are places of pilgrimage for lovers of Joyce. Beyond is Dalkey (that you will remember well) and eventually Bray Head. You can walk from Sandy Cove to Dalkey and up to the school in which Joyce taught, which figures in the novel as Summerhill, where the headmaster *"Dominie Deasy kens them a'*.

From Dalkey Village, the Vico Road runs a scenic route above the shoreline. You can look down to the lovely pebble beach at Killiney that we visited a number of times. It is on the Vico Road that Flann O'Brien set part of his wonderful novel the *Dalkey Archive*. It opens in a stately home called *Lawn Mower* (Mohr being Gaelic for large – hence large lawn). It proceeds to an underwater interview with St Augustine, examination of the theory of the exchange of molecules between policemen and their bikes, and a search for James Joyce who is reliably reported as being alive and tending a bar in Skerries. If Tim wants to read some short works which capture Irish wit and language, Flann O'Brien is a good place to start. *The Dalkey Archive* and *At Swim Two Birds* are my favourites.

If you walk the other way from your hotel, past Lansdown Road football ground, you can connect with Lower Baggot Street and walk into the city. You will come to the point where Baggot Street intersects with the Grand Canal. It is here that the friends of Paddy Kavanagh have put in place a park bench in his honour.

Kavanagh was a country lad from Monahan who came to Dublin in his mid-thirties and became the great poet of the Dublin Streets. He wrote a wonderful poem:

> *O commemorate me where there is water,*
> *Canal water preferably*
> *Greeny at the heart of summer. Brother...*
>
> *O commemorate me with no hero courageous*
> *Tomb – just a canal bank seat for the passer-by.*

There is another, grander memorial on the north side of the canal, with a bronze statue of the poet. But I prefer the simple granite and timber seat erected by his friends within months of his death. It is one of Dublin's small pleasures to eat fish from the old fashioned chipper on the adjoining street, while sitting on Patrick Kavanagh's canal bench.

You can proceed along Baggot St towards the city. While doing so you should recall Kavanagh's great poem of Dublin:

> *If ever you go to Dublin town*
> *In a hundred years or so*
> *Inquire for me in Baggot street*
> *And what I was like to know*
> *O he was the queer one*
> *Fol dol the di do*
> *He was a queer one*
> *And I tell you*

He may have had in mind his onetime friend Brendan Behan. Behan was a raconteur, novelist and playwright who came to represent a form of Irish nationalism and literature in the 1950s and 60s. He was imprisoned at the age of 16 in England as an IRA bomber and wrote some well-received plays including *The Quare Feller*, which was set in Mountjoy Jail. The song *The Aulde Triangle* comes from this play. In later years, he and Kavanagh fell out and Paddy would describe him as "the devil incarnate".

As you come towards the city centre you will see Merrion Square Upper on your right. Two blocks down is Merrion Square, at the centre of which is a wonderful garden that faces Leinster House, where the Irish Parliament or Dáil Éireann is located. Robbie Gilligan, Shane Butler and I used to walk twice around the gardens each lunch time. In the North West corner is a statue of Oscar Wilde sprawled languorously over a rock and looking towards the house opposite in which he was born. There are places surrounding the statue on which you can write your favourite Wildian witticism or aphorism.

If you continue along Baggot Street however you will enter St Stephen's Green. Before you do, on your left you will see Donohue's, the pub in which the Dubliners were formed. It is unchanged and while it has some passing tourists, it is a place for serious lovers of traditional music. Every Friday lunch time is the Civil Servant's Session, where some very accomplished musicians meet, away from *"counter and desk amid grey eighteenth century houses"* to share their music.

Stephen's Green is itself a wonder and I have spent many pleasant hours there, escaping the noisy city. It is also very historic. Michael Mallin and Constance Markievicz commanded a force during the 1916 rebellion which held the Green while being fired down upon from the Shelbourne Hotel located across the road. There is a bust of Countess Markievicz in one corner of the green, though you have to look for it.

St Stephens Green is at the top of Grafton Street that you know well. It figures also in song and literature. This from Kavanagh from *Raglan Road* that he wrote for the great Dublin beauty, Hilda Moriarty, with whom he was very much in love:

> *On Grafton Street in November we tripped lightly along the ledge*
> *Of the deep ravine where can be seen the worth of passion's pledge,*
> *The Queen of Hearts still making tarts and I not making hay -*
> *O I loved too much and by such and such is happiness thrown away.*

You know the shopping on Grafton Street well, so I won't go into that. On your left however, in Harry St, is McDaids, where Kavanagh, O'Brien (who also wrote under the pseudonym *Myles na gCopaleen* for the Irish Times), Behan, Anthony Cronin, J P Dunleavy, and other writers and journalists associated with the Irish Times held court during the 1940's and 50's. Dunleavy's novel *The Ginger Man* is believed to be based on Behan. McDaid's is an appropriate place of pilgrimage for a journalist Ell.

At the corner of Harry St and Grafton St Tim, is a bronze statue of Phyll Lynott of Thin Lizzie fame, referred to in Roddy Doyle's *The Commitments* as *"the first black man in Ireland."*

There are a number of pubs worth mentioning in the streets that run to the right between Grafton St and Kildare St. *Davy Byrne's* is the place to which the American tourists head because of its prominence in *Ulysses*. It retains no original features however and I would not recommend it. I would recommend *John Kehoe's* in South Anne St, however. As Sean O'Casey says in *The Plough and the Stars*:

"A pint of plain is your only man"

The quest for the perfect pint is the Dublin Grail.

Bewley's has a beautiful historic building but is not the place that it was. My favourite place for coffee or a meal in the south central area is *Dunne and Crescenzi's* in Lwr Frederick St, just off Nassau St. I think that they might have opened a second place in Sandymount.

With the takeover of Fred Hannah excellent bookshop in Nassau St (opposite the side entry to Trinity) I think that the best bookshop in the city centre is *Hodges Figgis* in Dawson St. It was founded in 1768 and is mentioned in *Ulysses* also. It has an excellent collection of Irish literature.

Along Kildare Street, which is two blocks to your right, from Grafton Street, is the cultural hub of Dublin. The National Museum holds the Tara Broach and many things of great beauty and antiquity. My favourite is the National Library. Ireland boasts some of the greatest writers in the English language including Swift, Sheridan, Congreve, Goldsmith, Wilde, Shaw, Yeats, Joyce, Beckett, Kavanagh, Doyle and Heaney. The library frequently has special exhibits of their work. Around the corner is the National Gallery, which has a great collection of works by Jack Yeats.

At the bottom of Grafton St is Suffolk St which has on either side of the street, *Avoca* (mum's favourite shop) and *Avery's*, the sports shop where Carl worked while he was in Dublin with Sam. Avoca stands out from the Irish knitwear and pottery shops along Nassau St which are pitched to the American tourists in that it has high quality Irish made clothing and other goods.

You must of course visit Trinity. It is a wonderful university which retains its historic beauty while providing quality modern teaching and research. If you walk in the main gates from College Green, you will find that the students are offering guided tours of the campus at a very small price. There are of course the long queues to see the Book of Kells. Robbie Gilligan's office is in the Education Building that looks across the lawns to the old library. Shane tells the story that Robbie caused a stir when Neil Jordan was making his film about Michael Collins with Liam Neeson. They were filming the scenes in the Dáil after the Treaty was offered in the round building in the for-court. The light from Robbie's office could be clearly seen in the background but he refused to turn it off because the place was for scholarly work which should not be interrupted for the production of entertainment. In O'Casey's words "a darlin' man".

Trinity is a spiritual home, and I have some pride in having a book in the library and having given a public lecture in the Jonathan Swift auditorium.

Trinity College, University of Dublin

Temple Bar, which is to the north of College Green is the entertainment centre and used to be taken over on weekends by drunken buck's parties from the UK. I don't know if that still happens. It has some good eating places; you will remember the Bad Ass Café and Fitzers, Ell, but the music is tourist fare only. My favourite places there are Claddagh Records at 2 Cecilia St, which sells the best traditional music and the James Connelly Bookshop – the bookshop of the Irish Communist Party.

If instead of crossing the Liffey, you continue along Dame Street, you will come to Christchurch, and to your left Patrick's Close, the surrounds of St Patricks Cathedral where Swift spent the later part of his life. You can continue on the same street to Thomas Street and St James Gate where the Guinness Brewery is located. You might recall the words of the song *Easy and Slow*:

> It was down by Christ Church that I first met with Annie
> A neat little girl and not a bit shy
> She told me her father had come from Dungannon
> And would take her back home in the sweet bye and bye
>
> And what's that to any man, whether or no
> Whether I'm easy, or whether I'm true
> As I lifted her petticoat, easy and slow
> And I tied up my sleeve for to buckle her shoe
>
> All down the way Thomas Street, down to the Liffey,
> The sunlight was gone, and the evening grew dark
> Along Whitemans Bridge, and by God in a jiffy
> My arms were around her, beyond in the park

The Park is the Phoenix Park which is just across the Liffey. It is one of the largest urban parks in Europe and houses the Dublin Zoo. In 1882 The Chief Secretary for Ireland (the British Cabinet minister with responsibility for Irish affairs), Lord Frederick Cavendish, and the Under-Secretary for Ireland (chief civil servant), Thomas Henry Burke, were stabbed to death with surgical knives while walking from Dublin Castle in the park. A small republican group called the Invincibles were responsible. This marked the emergence of the Irish Republican Brotherhood (IRB) as a significant force in republican politics.

If you continue in the same direction you will come to Kilmainham where the historic Kilmainham Gaol is located. The tour here is worth doing. The gaol is where Parnell was incarcerated and received Gladstone's Home Rule emissaries. After Parnell's disgrace and death, Gladstone remained true to his Home Rule commitments, which contributed in no small way to the split in the British Liberal Party. It is also the place in which the leaders of the 1916 rebellion were held before they were executed. It has the chapel in which Joseph Plunkett married his fiancé Grace Gifford the night before he was executed. The Stonebreakers Yard, where the executions took place is a stark monument to the 1916 martyrs. Their memory is celebrated in Yeats's poem Easter 1916, considered one of the great poems in the language:

> *I write it out in a verse -*
> *MacDonagh and MacBride*
> *And Connolly and Pearse*
> *Now and in time to be,*
> *Wherever green is worn,*
> *Are changed, changed utterly:*
> *A terrible beauty is born.*

Alternatively, you can cross the Liffey at Bridge St, a block on from Christchurch. You will pass the Brazen Head hotel on your left. This appears in all the US guide books and so is usually pretty crowded. It is reputed to have the oldest continuous licence in Ireland (not confirmed) and a place in which Lord Edward Fitzgerald met with co-conspirators to plan the 1798 rebellion (confirmed). When you cross the bridge, you come to the bottom of the Phibsborough Road which leads north to Glasnevin and Finglas. At the corner where the Phibsborough Road becomes the Finglas Road is Hedigan's Brian Boru Hotel which features in the Paddy Dignan funeral section of Ulysses. We have had some good meals there with our friends Robbie and Mary.

About 150 meters up the Phibsborough Road is Stoneybatter, a dog leg on the road which has three pubs side by side. You will recall the words of the song that I sang to you as a child and that has always since been your baby song *The Spanish Lady*:

> *I've wandered north and I've wandered south*
> *By Stoneybatter and Patrick's Close*
> *Up and around by the Gloucester Diamond*
> *And back by Napper Tandy's house.*
> *Old age has laid her hand on me*
> *Cold as a fire of ashy coals*
> *But where o where is the Spanish Lady,*
> *Neat and sweet about the soul?*

We used to have a drink and a song there at Mick Nolan's pub, The Belfry each Thursday evening when it boasted the best session going in Dublin. Jimmy Kelly, brother of Luke, a Dubliners original, is a greatly respected Dublin singer but can seldom be coaxed now to sing; unless of course mum is present, in which case he always sings *The Call and the Answer*:

> *You are the call and I'm the answer*
> *You are the wish and I am the way*
> *You're the music, I the dancer*
> *You are the night and I am the day*
> *You are the night and I am the day*

You can walk from here along the north bank of the Liffey back towards O'Connell St. Each short section of the Liffey Quay is separately named. You will walk along Inns Quay, Ormond Quay and Batchelor's Walk. As you come towards O'Connell St, you will come across a group of Italian restaurants. These were established by Jim Wallace, an eccentric Dublin entrepreneur who has a love of everything Italian and everything to do with soccer. He is also an outspoken radical who hung banners from his establishments on the Liffey proclaiming opposition to the invasion of Iraq in

2003. On the wall of the alleyway that separates two of the restaurants is a copy of Leonardo's Last Supper with the faces of prominent Irish people replacing those of the apostles. Sinead O'Connor is amongst them.

O'Connell Street is now largely cleared of traffic and is not the chaotic place it was. At the start of the street is the huge monument to Daniel O'Connor, "The Liberator", much loved by the Catholic Church because he led the campaigns to remove the penalties imposed on Catholics after the 1798 rebellion. I am more interested in the small statue a little further up the road, in honour of William Smith O'Brien. Smith O'Brien led the 1848 Young Ireland rebellion for which he was transported for a time to Tasmania. The rebellion itself was farcical but Smith O'Brien was a towering figure in mid nineteenth century Europe. I had a bit of a run in with Christopher Koch when introducing a reading of his *Out of Ireland* a few years ago. He depicted John Mitchell, the fieriest of the Young Irelanders, who was also transported to Tasmania as, in my view, a very sanguine revolutionary. He also caricatured Smith O'Brien as an effete timid pederast; a grossly unfair treatment.

A little further up the street is a statue of the Trades Union leader, Jim Larkin, who led the Transport Workers Union during the seven month lockout of unionists in 1913 and with James Connolly, formed the Irish Labour Party. The final lines of Kavanagh's poetic tribute to him are on the monument.

> *And Tyranny trampled them in Dublin's gutter,*
> *Until Larkin came along and cried*
> *The call of Freedom and the call of Pride,*
> *And Slavery crept to its hands and knees,*
> *And Nineteen Thirteen cheered from out the utter*
> *Degradation of their miseries.*

On your left is the General Post Office, where the Irish Republic was declared by Padraig Pearce on Easter Monday 1916. You can see the bullet holes and the marks of the British shelling on the columns.

Right proudly high over Dublin Town they hung out the flag of war
'Twas better to die 'neath an Irish sky than at Suvla or Sud-El-Bar
And from the plains of Royal Meath strong men came hurrying through
While Britannia's Huns, with their long range guns sailed in
through the foggy dew

The best music session in Dublin is still to be had at *The Teachers Club*, in Parnell Square. It is at the top of O'Connell Street, on the left hand side of the street, just past the Sinn Fein Shop. The building is not particularly well marked, and you need to enter and go straight up the stairs. There is a bar and sitting rooms at the top, and the most glorious music from the best traditional musicians in the country.

There is much else to see and do; and a good deal of good song and poetry to enjoy in Dublin. Enjoy it all Ell.

Section 5: *In Retrospect and Prospect*

> O, but my conscious fears,
> That fly my thoughts between,
> Tell me that she hath seen
> My hundred of gray hairs,
> Told seven and forty years
> Read so much waste, as she cannot embrace
> My mountain belly and my rocky face;
> And all these through her eyes have stopp'd her ears
> *Ben Jonson, On my Picture Left in Scotland.*

So where are we after 50 years? What has happened and what influence have we had?

Mutatis mutandis, omnia manent. The more things change, the more they stay the same.

Extraordinary changes have been effected in the provision of services in the community that enhance and improve the quality of the lives that we lead. In particular, the circumstances of the most vulnerable in the community have been immeasurably improved by the development of universal services like childcare and improved access to education and in the targeted services like family support and disability services support. But still the challenges persist, how to provide for growing numbers of people at risk, particularly the elderly and infirm, within a diminishing resource base, as the population ages and a smaller proportion is contributing through employment related taxation. Additionally, there is a sense that the social consensus is fraying and once marginal voices that opposed support for refugees and recognition of the harms of colonialism for Indigenous populations, are becoming louder and gaining greater prominence.

It is worth reviewing some of the policy areas covered in this collection of articles.

Broadmeadows is no longer the social frontier. Many of the old families grew old in the area and new communities have developed, largely from the later waves of immigration and humanitarian resettlement. Meadow Heights, in the north of the area is home to the largest middle eastern community in Melbourne. And the service infrastructure has changed. Broadmeadows Youth Shelter, where I worked had been set up in Pat Brown's home which she opened to take in homeless young people, is no more. But it has been replaced by a network of services and supports for families and young people. Broadmeadows Community Health Service, which we worked to establish in the mid-70s, is now part of DPV Health, one of Victoria's largest community health services, covering the northern suburbs of Melbourne.

Sharpie culture has long disappeared but the drug culture that replaced it has grown to greater strength. Some may argue that this has some of the elements of community and social support of the culture it replaced. I disagree. I see only exploitation and heartache. On a positive note, Victoria is recognised internationally as the home of harm minimisation (Portugal has perhaps now established primacy). More has been done here than in most places to provide real world responses to substance abuse. A stand-out example is the Supervised Injecting Facility in North Richmond. It has saved many lives.

The Royal Commission into Institutional Abuse confirmed the endemic nature of child abuse by priests and religious. The Catholic Church has been begrudging in its acknowledgement of the harms it has done. Nevertheless, it has paid a high price for its failures. The pews in most churches on a Sunday are all but empty, no doubt in part because of growing secularism, but also because the Catholic community understands that has been betrayed and can no longer trust in its authority. The Church has aggravated its failures by the abject way it has sought to deny just compensation for its victim/survivors. It has adopted one legal artifice after another in an attempt to preserve its assets.

Victoria's juvenile justice system has gone backwards over the past 25 years. Once considered among the world's best, it now has overcrowding in training centres, high rates of incarceration, high recidivism and poor outcomes for many young people. It has fallen victim to political cowardice and knee jerk reactions to adverse events. Draconian approaches to bail have meant that many young people will spend longer incarcerated on remand than they would if they received a Youth Training Centre sentence, time during which they are schooled in an anti-social or criminal lifestyle. Victoria's past experience, and that of other jurisdictions has shown that early intervention with young people at risk, diversion programs, incarceration as a last resort and attention to employment and educational opportunities that assist young people to structure their time, are likely to be much more successful than single focused correctional approaches. I worked briefly with one of the state's largest non-government organisations providing community based juvenile justice services however and I was shocked to see an almost complete absence of a therapeutic framework to guide intervention with young people at risk of offending. There had been little progress from when I first worked in the sector 50 years ago.

It is argued that "tough" policies are required to send a message that criminal behaviour will not be tolerated. The very worst basis for social policy is the "sending a message" rhetoric. You have to ask: "what is the message?", "Who is the audience?" and what impact do you expect to have from sending it?". The audience is not the young people who might be offending, but a conservative electorate that is fearful for its property and safety. The intention is to amplify that fear. This creates a circle of intentionality in which fear begets extreme policy responses which beget fear. In the words of King Lear "This way madness lies".

Disaster management is a hostage to the next major event that dominates community and government's attention. Each event has distinctive characteristics which tend to frame policy going forward. In the Ash Wednesday event(s), large numbers of people perished in cars fleeing the fires, often directed into danger by police who lacked sophisticated communications and in-time information. It led to a general directive to shelter in place, prepare individual disaster plans and avoid the roads. The Black Saturday fires in February 2009, in which 173 people died, had a ferocity greater than previously experienced and many people perished in homes which could not be protected. The policy response was to move towards an early evacuation model in which whole populations were to be encouraged to relocate prior to an anticipated catastrophic event.

The Royal Commission into the Black Saturday bush fire response was dominated by a charismatic QC assisting the commission who had no experience of emergency management but drew upon his army reserve experience. He emphasised command and control models of management that ran counter to previous experience in Victoria and counter to international experience. Disaster management, and particularly recovery management is a complex and multi-faceted phenomenon, that requires levels of collaboration and cooperation from parties outside lines of command. Effective management requires the development of relationships over time, an understanding of mutual capability and a willingness to work together. Most importantly it requires the empowerment of those directly affected by the disaster, to manage their own recovery. In the process of managing this major event and in consequence of the Royal Commission, recovery management was centralised in a Bushfire Authority. New personnel took three months to get up to speed, leaving local authorities waiting for much needed assistance. One of the most respected and experienced disaster managers in the country, Inspector Bruce Esplin, was moved aside and the regional planning and coordination networks that had developed and successfully coordinated multiple events, were allowed to atrophy.

It may well be that the changed focus towards early evacuation is the most appropriate response given what we know of the impact of global warming. We can expect more extreme weather and more intense disaster events. This will reduce the amount of time that individuals will have to adjust their plans for survival and they may be well advised to get out quickly and in advance of the event.

The state's Child Protection Program has continued to grow and continues to dwarf the resources that are committed to early intervention and support of families. It has become increasingly rule bound and process oriented. It is designed to mitigate risk; not so much risk to children (though staff genuinely seek to do this), but mitigation of risk to governments and regulatory organisations. It lacks a learning model whereby workers are encouraged to acknowledge errors in a blame free environment, and to learn from these in collaboration with their peers. I am amongst many who think that the child protection industry is at risk of losing sight of its end user; children and families.

During the period of my professional life there has been a major expansion of services for the vulnerable, the disadvantaged and the disabled. When I first went to North East Victoria in the early 80s, the only early childhood service in the region was one part time speech therapist at Wodonga Hospital. There is now a developed network of services thanks to the work of the early heroes of children's services, Shirley Rutherford, Helen La Naus and many others. The establishment of the NDIS has made an extraordinary difference to the lives of people with a disability. Previously getting support was a lottery. Success had little to do with need. Now the majority of people with a disability have an entitlement to the support they need to live the lives they choose in the community, and with dignity. The scheme is not without its problems. There are issues to do with finance, workforce, eligibility, and safety, but the entitlement to service outweighs all of these concerns.

The NDIS is in many ways the outworkings of the reforms in intellectual disability services that took place in Victoria in the 80s and 90s. A strong if flawed rights based legislation, a focus on individuated care planning, the replacement of large congregate care facilities with smaller more home like accommodation, and the beginnings of fund holding by consumers prefigured the NDIS. Critics of the replacement of institutions with smaller group living arrangements are correct in saying that the new services were also institutional in nature and failed to provide individually preferred arrangements, but they were an important step away from the often hellish conditions that people experienced in the institutions, and they provided a dramatic improvement in the quality of life for the residents.

Care for the mentally ill in Australia continues to be frustrated by the artificial disjunction between primary mental health (Commonwealth responsibility) and serious mental illness (State responsibility). An attempt to address some of the systemic issues in providing mental health services in Victoria was made by the Royal Commission into Victoria's Mental Health System. The commission made some worthwhile recommendations to improve care, particularly with respect to community based support and continuity of care. Implementation of the Commission's recommendations has largely stalled however because of Victoria's financial difficulties.

Of the things to which I have been able to contribute, in my professional lifetime, the closure of Mayday Hills Training Centre and the amalgamation of the Albury and Wodonga hospitals to create Albury Wodonga Health are things of which I am particularly proud. The Albury Wodonga community (larger than Bendigo and Ballarat) suffered for many years from fractured and diminished acute health care. It took twenty years of sustained effort to overcome institutional resistance and to create an organisational model and delivery system that can provide the acute care that is needed. I acknowledge my colleagues Joe McGirr and Geof Lavender who were critical partners in achieving the amalgamation of services. Again, the outcomes are not perfect and the hospital suffers from the infrastructure decisions of another time, but the platform is there now.

The workforce challenges in rural health continue. Some progress has been made, particularly with the Rural Generalist Pathways that are being developed in most States, which support the development of a rural medical workforce that addresses both primary care and procedural medicine. The Allied Health Rural Generalist Pathway may be similarly fruitful. There are some significant local innovations such as the Central West Queensland One Practice Model and the Swan Hill thin markets initiative, which address continuity of care as well as workforce issues.

I am particularly pleased to see the way the nurse practitioners have become embedded in the health care system in Victoria. This provides greater workforce flexibility, makes better use of our clinical resources and adds advance practice skills associated with prescribing, ordering diagnostics and admitting patients to our nursing workforce. We have also made some limited progress in introducing non-medical prescribing. It is to be hoped that we can go further in reducing vocational rigidities, particularly with physician assistants.

The Victorian health system however is in dire straits. The COVID pandemic had a devastating impact as staff struggled with personal illness and illness amongst friends and family, extended and under-staffed shifts and patient demand far in excess of capacity. Health care facilities were stretched to breaking point. Many people in clinical roles and management, burnt out and left. On top of this a financial crisis brought about by unprecedented supply chain disruption and interest rate rises that have reduced disposable income and discretionary spending, and hence state government revenue, has put pressure on the state budget and the availability of additional funding to support hospitals and health services. In order to address this crisis, the Health Department has attempted to impose spending restraint and have sought to save funds through amalgamations and governance changes. This has generated little or no resource savings but increased stress. There have been further loses of senior clinicians and experienced managers. Meanwhile, the sorts of changes associated with developing new models of care are not receiving attention.

There are very significant savings to be made in providing public health services, principally in the area of avoidable admission to hospitals. Whenever I am doing service planning for hospitals, my first step is to undertake a population health status review of the community. I invariably find that large numbers are admitted to expensive hospital care where this could have been prevented by timely and appropriate primary care intervention and well coordinated chronic care management. The opportunity is there, particularly with the development of digital health, to transform the way that care is provided in a way that both reduces cost and improves health outcomes.

And the government department(s) within which I worked for a large part of my career; the Departments of Community Welfare Services, Community Services Victoria, Human Services, Health, Families Communities and Safety? They have been aggregated and disaggregated. They have lost much of the founders vision and passion that was palpable in the late 70s and 80s and over time they have seen authority and responsibility drawn to central management and away from operational managers who understood the work. The regional infrastructure of the department was painstakingly constructed through the 1970s and 80s and provided a firm basis of knowledge and understanding that was able to manage services effectively and to inform policy. That structure has been largely dismantled. I found in my later years in the department that to draw attention to the fact that the organisation was spiralling downwards towards the inevitable end that was its incompetence in managing COVID lockdowns, was to be labelled arrogant, code for "does not know their place". The department(s) continue to be staffed by good people who want to do good things, but their structures and processes mean that they frequently lack the information, knowledge and experience to realise their goals.

Perhaps the greatest concern now in health management is concerned with public health. The COVID experience has demonstrated that social media can be manipulated to provide misinformation and disinformation that constitutes a very significant public health risk. The most outlandish nonsense was regularly promulgated by people with negligible actual knowledge or by bad actors whose concern was to undermine confidence in established medical knowledge. It is in this area that we have gone backwards most significantly over the past 50 years.

Social policy and social administration, like most things of value, must be approached in a sustained and loving way. Attending carefully, over time, and to the detail, is in my view, imperative. I am grateful that I was given the oppoutunity of doing this.

www.ingramcontent.com/pod-product-compliance
Lightning Source LLC
Chambersburg PA
CBHW040252170426
43191CB00019B/2389